# TRIUMPH OF THE IMAGINATION: THE STORY OF WRITER J. K. ROWLING

# TRIUMPH OF THE IMAGINATION: THE STORY OF WRITER J. K. ROWLING

Lisa A. Chippendale

Introduction by James Scott Brady,
Trustee, the Center to Prevent Handgun Violence
Vice Chairman, the Brain Injury Foundation

Chelsea House Publishers

Philadelphia

*Frontispiece: J. K. Rowling, author of the successful Harry Potter series.*

## CHELSEA HOUSE PUBLISHERS

EDITOR IN CHIEF  Sally Cheney
DIRECTOR OF PRODUCTION  Kim Shinners
PRODUCTION MANAGER  Pamela Loos
ART DIRECTOR  Sara Davis
EDITOR  John Ziff
PRODUCTION EDITOR  Diann Grasse
LAYOUT  21st Century Publishing and Communications, Inc.

First Printing

1 3 5 7 9 8 6 4 2

The Chelsea House World Wide Web address is
http://www.chelseahouse.com

Library of Congress Cataloging-in-Publication Data

Chippendale, Lisa A.
    Triumph of the imagination: the story of writer J. K. Rowling / Lisa A. Chippendale.
        p.   cm. — (Overcoming adversity)
    Contents: Bewitching fans—The story begins—Harry Potter, marriage, and motherhood—From penniless to published—Harry Potter takes off—The Goblet of Fire and beyond—A literary phenomenon—Harry Potter and the media empire.
    ISBN 0-7910-6312-7 (alk. paper)
    1. Rowling, J. K.—Juvenile literature. 2. Authors, English—20th century—Biography—Juvenile literature. 3. Potter, Harry (Fictitious character)—Juvenile literature. 4. Children's stories  Authorship  Juvenile literature. [1. Rowling, J. K. 2. Authors, English. 3. Women—Biography.] I. Title. II. Series.

PR6068.O93.Z58 2001
823'.914—dc21
[B]
                                                                2001047604

# CONTENTS

# OVERCOMING ADVERSITY

# ON FACING ADVERSITY

*James Scott Brady*

I GUESS IT'S a long way from a Centralia, Illinois, train yard to the George Washington University Hospital Trauma Unit. My dad was a yardmaster for the old Chicago, Burlington & Quincy Railroad. As a child, I used to get to sit in the engineer's lap and imagine what it was like to drive that train. I guess I always have liked being in the "driver's seat."

Years later, however, my interest turned from driving trains to driving campaigns. In 1979, former Texas governor John Connally hired me as a press secretary in his campaign for the American presidency. We lost the Republican primary to a former Hollywood star named Ronald Reagan. But I managed to jump over to the Reagan campaign. When Reagan was elected in 1980, I was "sitting in the catbird seat," as humorist James Thurber would say—poised to be named presidential press secretary. I held that title throughout the eight years of the Reagan administration. But not without one terrible, extended interruption.

It happened barely two months after the Reagan administration took office. I never even heard the shots. On March 30, 1981, my life went blank in an instant. In an attempt to assassinate President Reagan, John Hinckley Jr. armed himself with a "Saturday night special"—a low-quality, $29 pistol—and shot wildly as our presidential entourage exited a Washington hotel. One of the exploding bullets struck me just above the left eye. It shattered into a couple dozen fragments, some of which penetrated my skull and entered my brain.

7

The next few months of my life were a nightmare of repeated surgery, broken contact with the outside world, and a variety of medical complications. More than once, I was very close to death.

The next few years were filled with frustrating struggles to function with a paralyzed right side, struggles to speak and communicate.

To people who face and defeat daunting obstacles, "ambition" is not becoming wealthy or famous or winning elections or awards. Words like "ambition" and "achievement" and "success" take on very different meanings. The objective is just to live, to wake up every morning. The goals are not lofty; they are very ordinary.

My own heroes are ordinary folks—but they accomplish extraordinary things because they try. My greatest hero is my wife, Sarah. She's accomplished a lot of things in life, but two stand out. The first has been the way she has cared for me and our son since I was shot. A tremendous tragedy and burden was dropped unexpectedly into her life, totally beyond her control and without justification. She could have given up; instead, she focused her energies on preserving our family and returning our lives to normal as much as possible. Week by week, month by month, year by year, she has not reached for the miraculous, just for the normal. Yet in focusing on the normal, she has helped accomplish the miraculous.

Her other most remarkable accomplishment, to me, has been spearheading the effort to keep guns out of the hands of criminals and children in America. Opponents call her a "gun grabber"; I call her a national hero. And I am not alone.

After a seven-year battle, during which Sarah and I worked tirelessly to educate the public about the need for stronger gun laws, the Brady Bill became law in 1993. It was a victory, achieved in the face of tremendous opposition, that now benefits all Americans. From the time the law took effect through fall 1997, background checks had stopped 173,000 criminals and other high-risk purchasers from buying handguns, and the law has helped to reduce illegal gun trafficking.

Sarah was not pursuing fame, or even recognition. She simply started at one point—when our son, Scott, found a loaded handgun on the seat of a pickup truck and, thinking it was a toy, pointed it at Sarah.

Fortunately, no one was hurt. But seeing a gun nearly bring a second tragedy upon our family, Sarah became determined to do whatever she could to prevent senseless death and injury from guns.

Some people think of Sarah as a powerful political force. To me, she's the person who so many times fed me and helped me dress during my long years of recovery.

Overcoming obstacles is part of life, not just for people who are challenged by disabilities, illnesses, or tragedies, but for all people. No matter what the obstacle—fear, disability, prejudice, grief, or a difficulty that isn't likely to "just go away"—we can all work to make this world a better place.

*J. K. Rowling poses in King's Cross Station on July 8, 2000, with her new book,* Harry Potter and the Goblet of Fire, *in hand. Rowling's best-selling books have made her one of the wealthiest women in the United Kingdom. She once was a single mother on welfare, worrying about providing for her infant daughter.*

# 1

# BEWITCHING
# FANS

IT WAS NEARLY midnight on July 7, 2000, yet lights inside the Borders bookstore in Santa Fe, New Mexico, were blazing. Inside were droves of children and their parents, talking excitedly while they waited in line. Many of the children, both boys and girls, sported pointy wizard hats, black capes or robes, or lightning bolt tattoos on their foreheads.

Meanwhile, across the Atlantic Ocean, a similar crowd had gathered outside King's Cross Station in London, England. There, it was the morning of Saturday, July 8. Several hours later a blue Ford Anglia pulled up to the station. The doors opened, and out stepped a red-headed woman. As the crowd began cheering, she was besieged by flashbulbs from the cameras of a herd of journalists.

Anyone transported to the Santa Fe bookstore or King's Cross Station from a mere four or five years earlier would have been mystified as to what these lightning-bolt-tattooed children could have been waiting for. Was the Santa Fe Borders hosting a midnight

Halloween party in July? And who was the redheaded woman at King's Cross Station—was she a movie star or a member of the British royal family?

No. The truth is much stranger—the children in Santa Fe were waiting for a book, the most anticipated launch of a novel in literary history. And in Britain the crowds were cheering the arrival of J. K. Rowling, the author of that book. Once mesmerized by video games, television, and the Internet, these kids had fallen under a new spell—that of Harry Potter, boy wizard.

The release of *Harry Potter and the Goblet of Fire,* the fourth book of Rowling's astoundingly popular Harry Potter series, was a well-choreographed sensation. The British, American, and Canadian publishers—Bloomsbury, Scholastic, and Raincoast Books, respectively—released the volume simultaneously in all three countries on July 8, 2000, at 12:01 A.M. They printed a record number of books for a first printing—5.3 million copies.

The publishers had carefully stoked fans' curiosity for several months by refusing to reveal any information about Book Four. They even refused to send reviewers advance copies, and J. K. Rowling gave few prepublication interviews. The public knew only that the book would be the longest yet in the series—734 pages in the American version—and that an important character would die. The publishers didn't even release the title of the book until June 27, less than two weeks before the book's launch.

Bookstores in each country had to sign a strictly worded agreement not to display or sell the books before July 8. The only exception to the rule was giant Internet retailer Amazon.com, which was permitted to ship the books on July 7. To drum up excitement—as if that was necessary—Amazon offered its first 200,000 advance customers free next-day delivery on July 8, a Saturday, courtesy of a fleet of Federal Express planes and trucks. The ploy worked wonders. Amazon received 282,650 advance orders of the title, by far the most advance orders ever for a single book.

Like the Borders bookstore in Santa Fe, thousands of bookstores in Britain, the United States, and Canada had planned parties around the midnight release of the book, garnering hundreds of attendees and advance reservations for the volume. But of the thousands of Americans, Canadians, and Britons waiting in line, not all walked away satisfied. Some kids—and adults—left empty-handed as overwhelmed stores ran out of stock. Before the end of July the publishers printed several million more copies of the sought-after volume.

Midnight book-release parties were not the only sign of

*Children reach for copies of the latest Harry Potter book as they crowd an after-midnight July 8, 2000, book-release party. Fans all over the world participated in similar book-release events celebrating Rowling's latest work of fiction.*

Harry Potter's tremendous popularity. Rowling's arrival at King's Cross Station the morning of July 8 was not coincidental. She was there to take a ride on the Hogwarts Express, an old-fashioned locomotive Bloomsbury had rented and named for the fictional train that whisks Harry and his peers from Platform 9¾ at King's Cross Station to the Hogwarts School of Witchcraft and Wizardry. The real-life Hogwarts Express embarked from a specially built Platform 9¾, taking Rowling on a four-day whistle-stop publicity tour from London to Perth, Scotland. At every stop eager fans would have a chance to meet the author and have their books signed. However, to limit the crowds and attract even more publicity, Bloomsbury took a lesson from another children's classic, Roald Dahl's *Charlie and the Chocolate Factory*. As with the golden tickets found in Wonka candy bars that allowed access to the chocolate factory in Dahl's novel, only children who had won a special golden ticket via a drawing or contest at their local bookstore were allowed to participate in the book signings.

All this publicity was probably unnecessary; after all, 21 million Harry Potter books, in 35 different languages, were already in print before the fourth volume was released. True to predictions, *Harry Potter and the Goblet of Fire* soon joined the series' previous three installments at the top of the *New York Times* best-seller list for children's books. In fact, the existence of that list is a testament to the power of Harry Potter. The series would have dominated the top four slots of the *Times'* regular best-seller list if the paper had not created a separate children's list in July 2000 in response to complaints from publishers of adult fiction.

Millions of books in print. A feature film in the works. Children flocking to bookstores and begging their parents for a book that weighed several pounds.

Just who is Harry Potter, anyway?

For anyone who hasn't read the books—and who has been out of contact with television, newspapers, the Internet, radio, or any other form of news media for

several years—Harry Potter is a young, fictitious wizard, 10 years of age when the first book of the series begins.

As *Harry Potter and the Sorcerer's Stone* opens, Harry is unaware of his magical powers. For as long as he can remember, he has been living in a closet under the stairs in the home of his nasty aunt Petunia and uncle Vernon Dursley and his equally appalling cousin, Dudley. The Dursleys are what the wizarding world refers to as Muggles, or completely non-magical people. Harry is an orphan, both of his parents having been killed when he was an infant—supposedly in a car crash.

Harry soon discovers the truth—or the beginnings of it—during a birthday visit from a giant of a man named Hagrid, the groundskeeper at the Hogwarts School of Witchcraft and Wizardry. Not only is Harry a wizard by birth, but his parents died fighting the thoroughly evil

*More than 21 million Harry Potter books were in print in 35 different languages before the release of the fourth volume. Here executives of China's People's Literature Publishing House show off their new Chinese translations of the Harry Potter books.*

wizard Voldemort, who is so feared that other wizards refer to him only as You-Know-Who. Strangely, Voldemort was unable to kill Harry. His curse rebounded off the infant boy, vanquishing the evil wizard and leaving Harry with a scar in the shape of a lightning bolt.

Harry, so despised and neglected by the Dursleys, is famous in the magical world. Over the strenuous objections of his magic-fearing aunt and uncle, Harry leaves home to attend Hogwarts. There he must try to live up to the expectations that the magical community has for him, while dealing with typical preadolescent woes: unfair teachers, cruel bullies, and mountains of homework. That's not all, of course; Voldemort isn't really gone, and he still has it in for Harry Potter.

None of this breaks new ground in children's literature. So what is so special about these books that they transformed a generation of video-hooked kids back into readers? And why have they bewitched adult readers as well, who are responsible for purchasing at least 30 percent of the Harry Potter volumes?

Maybe it's magic—and it very well could be, as the books are full of the stuff. Although author J. K. Rowling draws on a wealth of tradition in fantasy literature, her magical world is bursting with unique and vastly entertaining detail. Hogwarts, in particular, is full of delights: There is a professor who is a ghost, not to mention a whole host of other ghosts ranging from mournfully friendly to nastily insane. Students are sorted into four in-school "houses" by a clever, singing, telepathic hat and have classes in Potions, Transformation, and Care of Magical Creatures. Photographic images—static and lifeless in our Muggle world—are changeable and always moving in the wizarding world. Sometimes the subject of a photograph even gets bored and wanders off. Mail is delivered by owls and may even occasionally include a loud verbal tirade from an outraged family member, called a Howler.

Plus, Rowling has an ear for names. The four houses at

Hogwarts have monikers that seem to reflect their attributes: Gryffindor (bravery), Hufflepuff (loyalty and hard work), Ravenclaw (intelligence and knowledge), and Slytherin (cunning and ambition). The wise, kind headmaster's name is Albus Dumbledore, and the unpleasant bully of the book is named Draco Malfoy, a name that just reeks of nastiness. Rowling even invented a magical sport: Quidditch, a cross between soccer and lacrosse, played in midair on flying broomsticks. She also has a nose for candy, a subject popular with children of all ages. There are Chocolate Frogs, which come with collectible wizard trading cards, and Bertie Bott's Every Flavor Beans—and Rowling means *every* flavor, including delicious ones like toffee and cinnamon, and disgusting ones like spinach and earwax.

In addition to her flair for names, Rowling also has a gift for the kind of silly humor kids love. Sometimes she uses it to poke fun at her characters. For example, Harry's unpleasant aunt Petunia is described as having "nearly twice the usual amount of neck, which came in very useful as she spent so much of her time craning over garden fences, spying on the neighbors." In other cases, humor simply pervades her descriptions, such as this one of Hogwarts School of Witchcraft and Wizardry: "There were a hundred and forty-two staircases at Hogwarts: wide, sweeping ones; narrow, rickety ones; some that led somewhere different on a Friday; some with a vanishing step halfway up that you had to remember to jump. Then there were doors that wouldn't open unless you asked politely, or tickled them in exactly the right place, and doors that weren't really doors at all, but solid walls just pretending."

Rowling's humor also exists on another level for adult fans, making it clear that her mission, beyond writing a children's book, is satire as well. Stodgy English private schools like Eton, where the students—all boys—are required to wear tailcoats, as if they were attending a prom, are a particularly favorite target. Early in Book One, Rowling describes the uniform Harry's cousin, Dudley, sports for his school, which

*J. K. Rowling signs a book for a fan. What has catapulted Rowling and her creation Harry Potter into the limelight? Perseverance, talent, luck, and perhaps a bit of magic.*

has the amusing name of Smeltings: "Smeltings' boys wore maroon tailcoats, orange knickerbockers, and flat straw hats called boaters. They also carried knobbly sticks, used for hitting each other while the teachers weren't looking. This was supposed to be good training for later life."

Hogwarts itself is a caricature of such schools. After all, its students are required to wear a rather silly costume: pointed hats and robes. Rowling also spoofs school mottoes with Hogwarts's *Draco Dormiens Nunquam Titillandus,* which means "Never tickle a sleeping dragon." As Rowling explained in an online interview, "Lots of schools have pointless mottos like 'Reach for the stars' or 'Persevere and endure'; I wanted something useful."

Yet amidst all this delightful, imaginative fun are stories that feature children at school, interacting with one another in ways that anyone who is or ever was a child can easily recognize. Cliques form. The children are often cowardly and cruel—some more often than others, of course—yet some have a tremendous capacity for bravery and kindness. Even the heroes of the book—Harry and his friends Ron Weasley and Hermione Granger—behave childishly at times, showing impatience, selfishness, and stubbornness. Yet their overall good nature wins out as they confront sinister, dangerous, and morally complex mysteries in every volume.

So there you have it. The books feature an entertaining and highly detailed setting, realistic yet unique characters with interesting personalities and relationships, humor silly enough for children yet sophisticated enough for adults, and carefully plotted mysteries that leave the reader guessing until the last few pages. Plus, they've received more publicity than any other children's books in history.

Yet many other equally wonderful books—for both adults and children—languish unread on library shelves every year. What catapulted Harry Potter and his creator, J. K. Rowling, into the international limelight?

Perseverance, talent, and a little luck. And perhaps a bit of magic.

*A crowd waves good-bye as J. K. Rowling leaves aboard the Hogwarts Express, a special train her publishing company rented in honor of the release of Book Four. Trains occupy a prominent place in Rowling's life and work. The Hogwarts Express carries Harry to school; the idea for Harry Potter occurred to Rowling during a train ride; and most important for Rowling, her parents met on a train.*

# 2

# THE STORY
# BEGINS

IT ISN'T SURPRISING that the Harry Potter books include a very important train—the Hogwarts Express, which carries Harry and the other wizarding students to the Hogwarts School at the beginning of every term. Trains have figured very prominently in the life of J. K. Rowling, Harry Potter's creator. The inspiration for Harry's character came to her on a train ride between Manchester and London. And if her parents hadn't been riding on a certain train that left King's Cross Station in 1963, J. K. Rowling might never have been born.

At age 19, Peter Rowling was heading north to Arbroath, Scotland, for a navy posting. On the train he met Anne, also 19, a member of the Women's Royal Naval Service. Commonly called Wrens, these women provided clerical and secretarial support for the navy at that time. Anne, too, was being posted in Arbroath. It was love at first sight, and soon Peter proposed to Anne—on another train. It wasn't long before the two were married in Scotland.

Shortly thereafter, the couple moved back to England, to Chipping

Sodbury, an oddly named town near Bristol. Peter had gotten a job at the nearby Rolls-Royce factory, where the company made airplane engines, and Anne was a lab technician. Bristol is a center of airplane manufacturing, located in southwestern England on a peninsula bordered by the English Channel, the Celtic Sea, and the Bristol Channel. The Bristol Channel is just north of Bristol and separates the peninsula from Wales.

On July 31, 1965, at Chipping Sodbury General Hospital, Anne and Peter became the proud parents of their first child, a girl. They named her Joanne Rowling. Two years later they added another girl to their family, Dianne, called Di. Joanne claims her earliest childhood memory is of her sister's birth, or rather the Play-Doh her father gave her to keep her occupied while her parents fussed over their new infant. Young Joanne knew exactly what to do with the Play-Doh—she ate it.

Anne and Peter fostered Joanne's interest in books and stories at an early age by reading to her. One of Joanne's earliest experiences with literature stemmed from a bout with the measles at age four. Her father read her *The Wind in the Willows,* by Kenneth Grahame, to keep her mind off her illness. It worked. In *Telling Tales,* an interview series by Lindsey Fraser, Rowling said, "I don't remember feeling ill at all." Her mother enjoyed reading even more than her father and was "never happier than when she was curled up, reading. That was a big influence on me." Soon Joanne was inventing stories for her younger sister.

At age six Joanne wrote her first story, about a rabbit named, appropriately, Rabbit, and her friends, including Miss Bee. In the story Rabbit gets the measles and her friends come to visit. (When asked about the story during a chat with fans on America Online [AOL], Joanne commented wryly, "I'm negotiating the film rights now, not.") She told interviewer Lindsey Fraser that the story was based on Richard Scarry's children's books, which she loved.

Around this time, Joanne's family moved twice, in less than a year—first to Yate, outside of Bristol, then to Winterbourne, on the other side of the city. In Winterbourne the Rowling sisters became close friends with Ian and Vikki Potter, who lived four houses away. The girls enjoyed dressing up as witches and concocting make-believe potions. (Not surprisingly, Rowling's favorite holiday is Halloween.) As for Ian, he loved practical jokes, such as booby-trapping his sister's bicycle and coating playthings with slime from tadpoles and slugs. In between jokes, potions, and pointy witch hats, Joanne often read stories to

*A street scene from Bristol, England. The Rowling family lived in the suburbs of Bristol, and Joanne's father worked in the city's airplane-manufacturing industry.*

her friends. Rowling says that the Potter family provided the inspiration for Harry's last name. And perhaps Ian Potter's antics served as the basis for Fred and George Weasley, Ron Weasley's twin brothers, who show a remarkable gift for mischief during their years at Hogwarts.

Like many other children, Joanne had a series of pets. Unfortunately, they were often a source of sorrow. She was crushed when her first dog, Thumper, had to be put to sleep. Several years later the family's pair of guinea pigs came to a brutal end in the backyard when they were eaten by a fox. "I remember the scene of carnage on the back lawn—it was *not* pleasant," she recalled in *Telling Tales.*

The family would remain in Winterbourne for only three years before moving again. In 1974 they relocated north, across the Bristol Channel, in Wales. Their new home was in the town of Tutshill, near Chepstow in the Forest of Dean. The setting was quite different from what Joanne and Dianne were used to; unlike the towns near urban Bristol, Tutshill was a small country village. Rowling's parents, both raised in urban environments, had dreamed of living in the country. Tutshill was perfect and provided an easy commute to her father's job at the Rolls-Royce factory.

Perhaps Tutshill was the basis for Rowling's love of spooky settings. A castle on a nearby cliff overlooked the village, and the Rowlings lived next door to the church— which meant they lived next door to a graveyard, too. Rowling says that she didn't mind the graveyard, adding in *Telling Tales,* "I still love graveyards—they are a great source of names." The family also lived near the river Wye, and Joanne and Dianne enjoyed clambering over the huge rocks near the river and exploring the countryside. One thing Joanne didn't like, however, was her new school.

The very first day of school in Tutshill was a disaster for young Joanne. Her teacher, Mrs. Morgan, gave her a math test, and she got every question wrong. Mrs. Morgan didn't ask Joanne if she had ever learned how to do fractions, which were the subject of the entire test. She just assumed that Joanne was stupid, and she put her in the "stupid row" at the far right of the classroom. It was, as Joanne herself noted later, "as far right as you could possibly get without sitting in the playground." Joanne later admitted in *Telling Tales* that her teacher had influenced the character of Professor Snape, the cruel Potions Master at Hogwarts who seems to hate Harry with an alarming passion. One thing that didn't influence the Harry Potter books, however, was the type of school Joanne attended. Unlike Harry, Joanne never went to a boarding school; all of her precollege education took place in public day schools.

Joanne, quiet and shy, had trouble making friends. She was often teased about her last name—pronounced "Rolling"—with nicknames such as Rolling Pin and Rolling Stone. Still, there was something she did enjoy at school—English classes. She loved to read, and she particularly enjoyed stories by Edith Nesbit, Noel Streatfield, Paul Gallico, C. S. Lewis, and Elizabeth Goudge. She read *Little Women,* by Louisa May Alcott, when she was eight years old, and she loved it. "I *was* Jo March for a few months," she later told Lindsey Fraser.

Joanne's two favorite characters from her childhood reading show her preference for heroes and heroines who—like Harry Potter and his friends—aren't always perfect. "Maria [in Goudge's *The Little White Horse*] . . . was a very interesting heroine—she wasn't beautiful, she was nosy, she had a temper. She was human, in a word, when a lot of girl characters tend not to be. I [also] really like Eustace in *The Voyage of the Dawn Treader,* by C. S. Lewis. He is a very unlikeable character who turns good," she said in an online chat at Barnesandnoble.com.

Joanne would later note that *The Little White Horse,* her favorite childhood book, influenced the world of Harry Potter perhaps more than any other book. The novel relates the tale of a recently orphaned girl who is shipped off to live with her father's cousin and finds that she is an heiress to a magical kingdom filled with fanciful creatures and characters. The relationship to the orphaned Harry Potter's discovery of his magical heritage is unmistakable. However, the books are quite different stylistically, with dramatically different plots. Goudge's book, written in 1946, reads very much like a fairy tale and is filled with heavy-handed moralizing, whereas Rowling's books depict a more realistic—although fantastic—world of moral ambiguity and authentically childlike behavior. Still, the books have one deliberate similarity: Goudge always included details about what her characters were eating. That made such an impression on young Joanne that she later used the same technique in her own books. From the meager crusts of bread tossed at Harry by Aunt Petunia to the mouthwatering holiday banquets at Hogwarts, Harry Potter readers get a healthy helping of food in every volume.

Eventually Joanne, often called simply Jo, made several friends at Chepstow, whom she regularly entertained with invented stories. After a while she managed to convince Mrs. Morgan that she wasn't completely stupid, and she was promoted to the second left-hand row. Unfortunately, this entailed trading seats with a friend of hers, which shrank her meager social circle for a time.

Despite the difficulties, Joanne successfully made it through primary school. Her love for writing continued to grow, and she even wrote a "novel"—really just a long short story—about seven cursed diamonds. Joanne later commented on the story during an online chat hosted by AOL, saying, "It lacks a certain something, like any believable characters or anything in terms of plot."

Rowling's next school was Wyedean Comprehensive School, which she entered in 1976. For the first few years Rowling was painfully shy. She was a bright, quiet kid with glasses who loved to read and who got good grades—perhaps a classic example of a kid American children would call a nerd. To make matters worse,

Joanne had no athletic talent and even managed to break her arm playing netball, a low-contact sport. Similar to the American game of basketball, netball requires that defending players stay three feet away from an attacking player with the ball. Although fast-paced and requiring skill, the game doesn't usually result in too many broken arms.

Joanne also discovered that she was hopelessly inept in "shop" classes like metalworking and woodworking. "Mum always kept a ridiculous flat teaspoon I made

*Joanne was a good student but was not very athletic. She managed to break her arm playing netball, an English low-contact sport similar to American basketball.*

which was useless, completely hopeless," she admitted to Fraser.

Still, Joanne had her writing. She also stayed close to her sister, Di, and slowly developed a group of friends. Her best and oldest friend, she has said, was Seán Harris, on whom she based Harry Potter's loyal and lovable sidekick, Ron Weasley. She also dedicated the second Harry Potter book, *Harry Potter and the Chamber of Secrets,* to Seán: "For Seán P. F. Harris, getaway driver and foul-weather friend." Seán's car, a blue Ford Anglia, also makes an appearance in the second book, whisking Harry and Ron to Hogwarts in midair after they miss the Hogwarts Express. In *Telling Tales,* Joanne said that she later realized how important that car had been in her adolescent life, trapped as she and her friends were in the dull countryside. "Harry was rescued by that car, just as the car rescued me from my boredom," she explained.

Over time Joanne became more confident socially. She replaced her glasses with contact lenses and began asserting herself in class. She still kept most of her writing to herself, however, and she told no one of her desire to be a writer— not even Miss Shepherd, her favorite English teacher. Joanne admired Miss Shepherd for her firm but clear and enthusiastic approach, and she kept in touch with the teacher long after graduating from Wyedean. But Joanne did share a few of her stories with her sister and her friends, many of which featured them as valiant heroes.

As always, Joanne was an avid reader. She had been devouring Ian Fleming's James Bond novels since age nine, and not long after that she became a huge fan of Jane Austen, the author of *Pride and Prejudice.* "I find her un-put-downable," she said in an online chat at Scholastic's website. When Joanne was 14, her great-aunt Ivy gave her a book called *Hons and Rebels,* by Jessica Mitford. "It changed my life," Joanne later said. Mitford was an activist who fought in the Spanish Civil War in the 1930s. After the war she and her husband came to the

*Reading the books of Jessica Mitford, a muckraking journalist, labor activist, and champion of racial equality, changed Rowling's life. Mitford (pictured here) became her lifelong heroine.*

United States. Unfortunately, her husband died in World War II. Mitford remarried and went on to become a labor activist, a champion of racial equality, and a muckraking journalist who exposed the evils of the American mortuary business. *Hons and Rebels,* published in 1960 and called *Daughters and Rebels* in the United States, is Mitford's autobiography. Mitford would become Joanne's lifelong heroine.

Joanne did have other interests besides reading and writing. Despite her family's poor track record with pets, Joanne had become an enthusiastic collector of tropical fish, a hobby she continues to this day. She also liked drawing, and she wasn't as shy about sharing her art with others as she was about her writing. As for entertainment, Jo didn't see many movies, since Chepstow lacked a cinema and her family rarely watched television. However, she loved the theater. Her parents had taken her and her sister to several shows in London when they were young, but it wasn't until Joanne was in sixth form— the final year of secondary school—that she saw her first real play: Shakespeare's *King Lear.* "I was absolutely electrified by it," she remembered in *Telling Tales.* She attended plays as often as she could after that, and notes that Shakespeare's *The Winter's Tale* was her first encounter with an interesting name she never forgot: Hermione.

In 1980 the Rowling family received grim news when Joanne's mother, Anne, was diagnosed with multiple sclerosis at age 35. Multiple sclerosis is a progressive disease of the central nervous system. During the beginning stages of the disease patients suffer from a variety of symptoms, including reduced coordination, numbness, and shooting pain. Although there is no cure for the disease, patients usually live close to a normal life span, but most gradually deteriorate, ending up with at least partial disability.

Despite her concerns about her mother's illness, Joanne continued to excel in school. She did quite well on the mandatory tests required for graduation, then called O-levels but now referred to as GCSEs (General Certificate of Secondary Education). She received A's on her English GCSEs, but only a C on her physics test. However, she was quite pleased with that mark because, as she admitted in an online chat at Comicrelief.com, "I didn't understand Physics at all and still don't."

Joanne's newfound social confidence and stellar grades even earned her an appointment as Head Girl in her final year at Wyedean Comprehensive, a position that many of the female students aspired to. Although the position was largely ceremonial, Rowling remembers one aspect of the job that terrified her: she had to give a speech in front of her entire class. She managed to muddle through her speech and went on to graduate with high honors in 1983. She was pleased to be finally rid of Wyedean's atrocious brown-and-yellow uniform and has since steadfastly avoided wearing either color.

Now that she had graduated from secondary school, it was time for Joanne to plan for the future. Most 18-year-olds have no idea what they want to do with their life. Not Joanne. She knew exactly what she wanted to be: a writer. But she was plagued with self-doubt, worrying that her writing wasn't good enough. She had shared only a few stories with her sister and her friends, her shyness and fear of rejection keeping her from showing her work to her teachers or parents.

Joanne's parents knew nothing of her ambitions, and Joanne never worked up the courage to tell them. Anne and Peter, knowing their daughter's love of literature but hoping she would pursue a more practical course of study, pushed Joanne to major in French and classics at the University of Exeter. Exeter was located back across the Bristol Channel in the middle of England's south-western peninsula. The Rowlings predicted that studying a foreign language would improve Joanne's chances of landing a good job upon graduation.

Joanne took her parents' advice and enrolled at Exeter. She enjoyed her time there, although at first she was disappointed that the school wasn't the hotbed of radical protest she had expected. She had hoped to participate in social activism like her heroine, Jessica Mitford. Still, she was on her own at last, was doing fairly well in her classes, and had met her first boyfriend. She particularly

*Joanne enrolled in the University of Exeter (pictured). Her parents did not know of Joanne's dream of becoming a writer. They did know of her love for literature and encouraged her to major in French and classics.*

enjoyed the year she spent abroad in Paris as a teaching assistant. During her college years, Joanne continued to write but couldn't bring herself to show her work to anyone or submit it for publication. She also began a related hobby—collecting odd names. She found her classics courses particularly helpful in this pursuit, and she began filling notebooks with names derived from mythology and classic literature. She also jotted down odd names anytime she ran across them, whether they were "names from saints, place-names, war memorials, [or] gravestones." Of course, some of the names in her books she just plain invented.

Perhaps her writing and her name collecting distracted Rowling from her schoolwork. She did reasonably well at

Exeter, but she did not gain the academic honors she had won in high school. Although she did graduate in 1987 with a degree in French and classics, it was a mere 2.2, or average, degree. That seemed unimportant, however, as Joanne wrestled with how to plan for her future. What should she do next? She had no interest in a mundane job in an office. She just wanted to write.

*London, England's capital and largest city. After college Rowling moved here and became a secretary. She later admitted, "I proved to be the worst secretary ever." Instead of taking notes at meetings or writing letters, she was scribbling story ideas.*

# 3

# HARRY POTTER, MARRIAGE, AND MOTHERHOOD

EVEN THOUGH WRITING was Joanne's primary goal, she also had to eat. Writing wasn't going to pay the rent, especially since Joanne had not yet worked up the courage to send any of her stories out for publication. She was going to have to get a job. To improve her prospects, she went to London and took a course for bilingual secretaries. She freely admits now that this was a mistake, saying in *Telling Tales,* "Me as a secretary? I'd be your worst nightmare." The course did have one valuable aspect—Rowling learned to type. This skill would come in handy later, as she had to type up several copies of the first Harry Potter book for submission.

When she finished the course, Joanne had no choice but to don a suit and begin taking job interviews. She hated them. They seemed pointless, since they had nothing to do with her ambitions. She was only looking for a job to pay the bills while she wrote in her spare time. Despite her lack of interest, she found a position as a secretary. She moved to South London, where she shared a flat—the British name for an apartment—with a friend in the Clapham area.

Unfortunately, not only did Joanne dislike working as a secretary, she wasn't very good at it. She later admitted, "I . . . proved to be the worst secretary ever." First of all, she wasn't very organized. Even worse, she couldn't keep her mind on the job. Instead of taking the minutes at meetings, she scribbled story ideas onto her notepad. She typed up the stories at her desk instead of doing her work.

For Joanne this was the first in a series of uninteresting secretarial jobs. She didn't last very long in any of them. Sometimes she was fired because her bosses were not amused by her writing fiction while on the company clock. Other times she quit in disgust over the mind-numbing drudgery of the work. Her self-described worst job was as a temporary secretary for a surveillance company. They made products like bugs for telephones and infrared binoculars for spying on people at night. During an online chat at Barnes and Noble's website, Rowling described her time at the company: "I spent the whole time reading the catalogue. They were very creepy people. The products were very interesting, but the people were quite horrible." The only thing that interested Joanne was the novel she was working on, which she squeezed in during her lunch hour at area pubs and cafés.

Eventually Joanne found a more meaningful job: working at Amnesty International, researching human-rights abuses in French-speaking Africa. She was pleased that, like her heroine Jessica Mitford, she was helping to stand up for human rights. In *Telling Tales* she said, "If I wasn't writing full-time it was important that my time was being spent on something worthwhile."

After a few years, however, Joanne had to make a decision. Her boyfriend from college was moving to Manchester, and he asked her to come with him. She agreed. The decision would have a huge impact on her life. In 1990, after spending the weekend with her boyfriend looking for an apartment in Manchester, she took a train back to London. It was on

the long journey between the two cities, delayed due to mechanical problems, that she met Harry Potter.

"Harry Potter strolled into my head fully formed," Rowling told Paul Gray, a *Time* magazine reporter. As she looked idly out the train's window, watching some cows grazing in the English countryside, she suddenly had a vision of a boy with unruly black hair, green eyes, and round glasses. She knew he was a wizard—but she also knew that Harry didn't know what he was. The idea

*During a long rail journey between Manchester and London, Harry Potter, in Rowling's words, "strolled into my head fully formed." As soon as she arrived in London, Rowling ran home to begin work on the first book.*

intrigued her, and she grabbed for a pen to jot down some notes about her wizardly visitor. She quickly discovered she didn't have a working pen with her. She spent the rest of the train ride mulling over Harry and a school of magic, Hogwarts, in her head, soon coming up with the characters of Ron and Hagrid as well as several of the ghosts that haunt the school.

She spent much of her energy detailing Hogwarts, trying to imagine the school, the castle that housed it, and the subjects that budding young witches and wizards would learn. Right from the beginning she knew that she wanted a series of seven books, one for each year that Harry spends at Hogwarts.

When the train reached King's Cross Station, Joanne rushed back to her apartment for a working pen and a notebook. She was soon making lists, including character names and the seven subjects taught at Hogwarts.

From then on Harry Potter was the focus of almost all Joanne's thoughts. She dropped her other writing projects—including two nearly completed novels, both for an adult audience—to focus on the new book. She carefully developed names and histories for the characters, even those that would not appear until later books, and figured out the plots of all seven volumes. And then she started writing *Harry Potter and the Philosopher's Stone,* the series' first book.

She soon knew that Harry was an orphan, his parents having been killed in a battle with an evil wizard that she would name Voldemort. She gave Harry a mysterious souvenir from this battle, a scar shaped like a lightning bolt. Later, in an online chat on AOL, she explained her choice of a lightning bolt shape: "It had to be something that suggested the intensity of the pain that Voldemort was trying to inflict upon him but a simple and plausible shape for a scar."

Meanwhile, she completed her move to Manchester and began sharing an apartment with her boyfriend. She landed another dull job, this one with the Manchester Chamber of Commerce. It didn't last long. Her position

*Harry Potter (pictured) is an orphan; his parents were killed in a battle with an evil wizard named Voldemort. Harry wears round glasses and sports a lightning-bolt-shaped scar— a mysterious souvenir of that fateful battle with Voldemort.*

was eliminated shortly after she began working there. Luckily, she soon got another job as a secretary at the University of Manchester.

Joanne's excitement about the developing world of Harry Potter was soon dampened by a host of personal problems. Only a month after Joanne moved to Manchester, her mother finally succumbed to multiple sclerosis. Anne Rowling was only 45 at her death. Joanne was crushed by the loss, and stunned. Intellectually she had known that her mother's condition was worsening—her mother had been wheelchair-bound for the last several years—but she hadn't given it much thought. Later, in an interview in the April 18, 2001, issue of the *London Guardian,* she said, "The last time I saw her before she died, I went back for Christmas. I can't believe in retrospect that I didn't really realise what was about to happen because she was so ill. Her mobility was very limited; she looked ill, very ill—which I'd never really seen before. She was absolutely exhausted."

Joanne deeply regretted that she had never shared her fiction with her mother. She had never even told her that she wanted to be a writer, and Anne knew nothing of Harry Potter's sudden appearance in Joanne's life. Rowling's grief over the loss of her mother would later come out, unconsciously, in a passage in *Harry Potter and the Philosopher's Stone* in which the orphaned Harry sees his parents and the rest of his family in a magical mirror: "The Potters smiled and waved at Harry and he stared hungrily back at them, his hands pressed flat against the glass as though he was hoping to fall right through it and reach them. He had a powerful kind of ache inside him, half joy, half terrible sadness."

This passage isn't an aberration. Death and dying are major themes in the Harry Potter books. Harry's parents were murdered, his mother dying to save his life. And Harry's nemesis, Lord Voldemort, has devoted much of his power to finding ways to thwart death and achieve eternal life. Plus, Harry's life, and those of his friends, is regularly threatened throughout the series.

The months after her mother's death were difficult for Joanne. She and her boyfriend weren't getting along. Once they had a fight so huge that Joanne stormed out of their apartment, ending up at a local pub, then a Manchester hotel. The fight did produce some useful results, however. Luckily Joanne had a pen and a notebook with her, and she spent the evening inventing Quidditch. She knew she wanted a special wizardly sport, and for some reason she knew it needed to begin with a *Q.* She wrote down word after word that began with the letter until she stumbled on Quidditch, which she loved immediately, circling it five times on the page. She then filled the notebook with diagrams of the playing field, as well as names for the game's positions and its three types of balls: the Snitch, the Quaffle, and the Bludger.

As if grief over her mother's death and fights with her boyfriend weren't enough, Joanne's apartment was burglarized a short time later. The thieves stole nearly everything her mother had left her. Although her family and friends were supportive, Joanne knew it was time to make a change in her life.

Trying to decide what to do next, Joanne thought about the year she had spent in Paris as a teaching assistant. She'd enjoyed the work. Perhaps she would find happiness working overseas as an English teacher. It didn't seem an unreasonable step. After all, neither her relationship with her boyfriend nor her career as a secretary seemed to be working out. The only thing that mattered to her was Harry Potter, and he was portable.

In 1991, Joanne got her wish. She found a job as a teacher of English as a second language in Oporto, Portugal. Nervous but determined to give teaching a try, Joanne said good-bye to her father, sister, and friends and packed her bags for Portugal. On her flight to Oporto, Joanne thought of the names for the four houses at Hogwarts: Gryffindor, Hufflepuff, Ravenclaw, and Slytherin. Having no paper with her, she jotted the names down on the back of an airsickness bag. "Yes, it was empty!" Rowling noted in an interview on Amazon's United Kingdom website.

Although she was homesick at times, Joanne quickly settled into her new life. She taught in the afternoons and evenings, which left her mornings free for writing. And write she did: looking for perfection, she scribbled 10 different versions of the first chapter of *Philosopher's Stone*. Happily, Joanne discovered that she enjoyed teaching. She had students of nearly every age, from 8 to 62,

although the majority were teenagers. Most of them were
learning well, and the school administration was happy
with her, even making Joanne head of the department. In
fact, there was quite a bit she liked about Portugal—the
sunny, warm weather; the friendly people—but not tripe,
the Portuguese delicacy made from the stomach of oxen
or cattle. That made the top of her list as her least favorite
food. But soon she found something else to add to her
happiness: romance.

Six months after arriving in Portugal, Joanne met Jorge
Arantes, a handsome journalist who worked for a television station. They dated and fell deeply in love. Within a
few months of their first date the two were married.

Joanne was blissfully happy, and she was making
progress on the Harry Potter book. Unsure at first whether
the books should be for children or adults, she settled on
just writing a story that she would want to read, choosing
not to worry about the target age. The humor that pervades
the novel is based on what Joanne found funny, not what
she thought would amuse children or other adults. Joanne
also made an art form of naming her characters, picking
monikers that amused her or seemed to suit the character's
personality or mannerisms. In an interview with Stories on
the Web, Rowling explained the origin of the names of
two important characters: the kind, wise headmaster of
Hogwarts, Professor Dumbledore, and Harry's clever and
loyal white owl, Hedwig. "'Dumbledore' is an Old English
word meaning bumblebee, and 'Hedwig' a medieval saint."
Rowling explained that she chose *Dumbledore* because
she could imagine the headmaster humming to himself
as he walked the halls of Hogwarts, like a bee buzzing
around a flower. To temper the humor, she also included
a serious, dark side in the book—the pure evil of the
wizard Voldemort, who threatens Harry and Hogwarts.

Still, Joanne eventually realized that a book featuring a
child protagonist and filled with magic would be considered
primarily a children's book. She wanted her characters to

behave in ways that young readers would find realistic and familiar. Luckily, she discovered that even though she had never tried her hand at children's stories or books before, she could easily "think [herself] back to 11 years old." That made it very easy for her to create the character of Hermione, Harry's know-it-all friend. Hermione, Rowling said in an interview with *Salon* magazine, "is based almost entirely on myself at the age of 11." She explains that Hermione's insistence on academic perfection—an

*Oporto, Portugal, where Joanne found a job as an English teacher after a series of personal setbacks prompted her to seek a change in her life.*

*Rowling (shown here talking with children at a book signing in Chicago) used her vivid memories of her childhood to shape Harry's world. She based the character Hermione almost entirely upon herself at age 11.*

annoyance to her classmates—is really just her way of hiding her insecurity. Rowling notes, however, that Hermione is much more clever than she was, and more annoying—she hopes.

As Joanne scribbled out page after page of her novel, she was enjoying her time with Jorge, although it was limited because he worked a very demanding schedule. Then, in 1992, Joanne discovered she was pregnant. She was excited at first, but soon became increasingly distressed as Jorge's long work hours kept them apart. She needed support during the hormonal and emotional changes brought on by pregnancy, especially while she was trying to juggle teaching and writing. Still, she kept working on the book, and as summer 1993 neared, she had finalized the first three chapters and written a rough draft of most of the rest of the book.

Joanne was thrilled when Jessica was born in 1993, not long before her 28th birthday. "That was, without doubt, the best moment of my life," she told interviewer Lindsey Fraser. She named her daughter after her favorite Jessica: writer-activist Jessica Mitford. Unfortunately, things soon took a turn for the worse. Jorge and Joanne weren't getting along, and Joanne grew increasingly frustrated and depressed. Finally, she realized she was no longer in love with Jorge. Not long after Jessica's birth, the couple split up for good, and they eventually divorced.

Joanne had suffered another devastating loss. Now she was a single mother with a daughter to support, and she felt abandoned and alone. She didn't feel her job was secure, and she was worried about supporting her daughter during the summer months, when her job stopped. She began to think about leaving Portugal. She feared it would continually remind her of her failed marriage, and she had no family and few close friends in the foreign country.

Thankfully Joanne received a call from her sister, Dianne, who was studying law in Edinburgh, Scotland. Di suggested that Joanne come to Edinburgh so she would be near family while she tried to pick up the pieces of her life.

So Joanne packed up her belongings again, took her baby daughter, and flew to Edinburgh for the 1993 Christmas holidays. She was careful to bring all of her Harry Potter work with her; the pages filled half a suitcase. She was alone and had no idea how she was going to support herself and Jessica. But she was certain of one thing—she wasn't going to abandon Harry Potter.

*The first month back in the United Kingdom was hard for Joanne. She was worried about providing for her daughter and took Prime Minister John Major's cutting remarks about single mothers to heart.*

# 4

# FROM PENNILESS
# TO PUBLISHED

JOANNE WAS HAPPY to see Dianne. However, the Christmas holidays still seemed bleak to her because she was worried about providing for her daughter. As if she weren't feeling bad enough about her situation, one month after her return to the United Kingdom, Prime Minister John Major made a speech that sharply criticized single mothers. He blamed them for many of society's ills and implied that women on public assistance were lazy, purposefully avoiding work.

Joanne hadn't planned to stay in Edinburgh. Now she had a decision to make. All she really wanted to do was write about Harry Potter—but Harry wasn't going to pay the rent or buy food for Jessica. After all, the young wizard's personal fortune of golden Galleons and silver Sickles was locked up in a vault and guarded by goblins in the wizards' bank, Gringotts—all of which was stuck inside Rowling's head. She considered going to London, where she had several friends, to look for a job.

Luckily, something happened to help her make up her mind. She told the story of Harry Potter to Dianne, who had been listening to Joanne's stories since the two were toddlers. Di loved it. Di's support gave Joanne the confidence finally to overcome her fear of making her work public. She decided that it was now or never for Harry Potter. She would spend one year finishing *Harry Potter and the Philosopher's Stone,* then she would submit it for publication. During that year she also planned to work on obtaining a postgraduate certificate in education so she would be eligible to teach in Britain.

Joanne knew she couldn't stay with her sister forever, but she wanted to live in Edinburgh. She liked the city; it seemed a pleasant place to raise a child, and it was small enough that she would be able to walk around most of it and avoid paying bus fare. Joanne put a deposit on a small two-room apartment in Edinburgh. Although the apartment lacked heat, it came with complimentary mice.

Joanne felt defeated, however, when her hope of working part-time to make ends meet was thwarted by the British system of public assistance, the equivalent of welfare. Although Rowling was eligible for public assistance, she was not eligible for child care if she worked. She was forced to remain unemployed and live entirely on public assistance.

Joanne was deeply ashamed of having to accept government charity and found that some acquaintances now avoided her. She was also frustrated that she was such a poor provider for Jessica. Once, after visiting a friend of her sister's who had recently had a child, she realized that where her friend's son had a bedroom full of toys, Jessica's playthings would fit in a shoe box. "I came home and cried my eyes out," she said in an interview in the July 8, 2000, issue of the *London Guardian.* During the time she spent on assistance—about six months—Joanne battled depression, for which she underwent counseling. Her later recollections of that period formed the basis of the sinister and terrifying dementors in the third Harry Potter book, *Harry Potter and the Prisoner of Azkaban*. The dementors are cloaked, gaunt, eyeless creatures who feed on human misery, living for the grim pleasure of sucking out the souls of condemned wizards. In the book, the relationship of the dementors to depression is made clear by Professor Lupin, who teaches Defense Against the Dark Arts, in a conversation with Harry:

> Dementors are among the foulest creatures that walk this earth. They infest the darkest, filthiest places, they glory in decay and despair, they drain peace, hope, and happiness out of the air around them. Even Muggles feel their presence, though they can't see them. Get too near a dementor and every good feeling, every happy memory will be sucked out of you. . . . You'll be left with nothing but the worst experiences of your life.

Perhaps the difficulties in Joanne's life were the source for one of the series' key themes: loneliness. Joanne understood the pain of being alone that children feel so keenly when they are rejected or ostracized by family members or friends. Harry, at the beginning of the book, is rejected by everyone. The Dursleys, who are the closest things to parents that Harry has, don't even try to hide their distaste for their odd nephew and their preference for their son, Dudley. Early in the first book, Joanne writes, "Every year on Dudley's birthday, his parents took him and a friend out for the day, to adventure parks, hamburger restaurants, or the movies. Every year, Harry was left behind with Mrs. Figg, a mad old lady who lived two streets away. Harry hated it there." And when Harry receives his first letter from Hogwarts one chapter later, Joanne makes it clear that he is alone: "Harry picked [the letter] up and stared at it, his heart twanging like a giant elastic band. No one, ever, in his whole life, had written to him. Who would? He had no friends, no other relatives."

Once Harry gets to school, things change, but the theme of loneliness persists. After a nighttime escapade by Harry and his friends loses Gryffindor 150 points in the House Cup standings—dropping them into last place from first in Hogwarts's yearlong interhouse competition—Harry is ostracized: "From being one of the most popular and admired people at the school, Harry was suddenly the most hated. . . . Even Quidditch had lost its fun. The rest of the team wouldn't speak to Harry during practice."

Joanne managed to overcome her feelings of hopelessness and continue writing her book. During this time she was nearly broke. Public assistance provided only about $105 a week, barely enough for Joanne to pay her rent and buy food for herself and Jessica. Experiencing the tremendous difficulty of making ends meet on such a pitiful sum of money, Rowling found Prime Minister Major's earlier tirade against single mothers even more galling. "I had no intention, no desire, to remain on benefits. It's the most soul-destroying thing. I don't want to dramatise, but there were nights when, though Jessica ate, I didn't. The suggestion that you would deliberately make yourself entitled . . . you'd have to be a complete idiot," she later said to reporter Helena de Bertodano during an interview for the *London Telegraph*.

Despite being unemployed, Joanne had little opportunity to write. Her infant daughter required almost constant care, and she hated writing in her freezing, gloomy apartment. She didn't give up, however. She just found a creative solution. Every day she put Jessica in her baby carriage and walked around Edinburgh until Jessica fell asleep. Then she would head for a local café, buy a cup of espresso and a glass of water, and write for a few hours while Jessica slept nearby.

*Joanne made it a point to get out of her freezing, gloomy apartment each day. She wrote in local Edinburgh cafés like the one pictured here while her infant daughter slept nearby in her baby carriage.*

Not all café owners appreciated her sitting for hours in their establishment, having ordered only one cup of coffee. Joanne began to frequent Nicolson's Café, a new coffeehouse partly owned by her brother-in-law. The staff was kind to her and let her sit for hours, nursing her coffee and her water as she painstakingly churned out page after page of Harry Potter's story in longhand. When she ran out of paper, she would scribble her ideas on napkins.

Joanne continued to revise relentlessly. In fact, she later admitted in an interview for BBC Online that only once did she write a chapter completely right the first time through. "That was the chapter in *Philosopher's Stone* when Harry learns to fly. I remember vividly—the old story we've heard a million times—my daughter fell asleep, it was a beautifully sunny day, I sat in a café, and wrote that chapter from beginning to end. And I think I changed two words."

After nearly a year Joanne finished her manuscript and began the long process of typing it. She used a cheap manual typewriter, which she had scrimped to buy for $63, or the computer lab at the college where she was taking her teaching classes. "I was terrified that people would discover that I wasn't doing my course work," she said in *Telling Tales.* She had to type up two copies of the manuscript because she didn't have any spare money for photocopying it, which would have cost quite a bit. A typical children's novel is about 40,000 words—and *Harry Potter and the Philosopher's Stone* was twice that long.

Finally, in 1995, after five years of writing and rewriting, Joanne was finished with the novel. She could hardly believe it. Now it was time to take the next step: getting published. After spending some time in the library looking up agents and publishers, Joanne chose one of each. Swallowing her fear and nervousness, she sent her two copies of the manuscript off and settled in to wait for a reply. With the immense project finished, Joanne found a typing job and completed her teaching certification. Not long after that, she landed a part-time job teaching French. She was thrilled to be off public assistance. She enjoyed teaching again, although she had to put up with a bit of teasing about her last name. Her students liked to serenade her with the theme song from the 1960s American television show *Rawhide* ("Rolling, rolling, rolling, keep those wagons rolling . . . "). They also poked fun at her English accent.

After weeks of waiting, Joanne was disappointed when she received both copies of her manuscript back with rejection letters. Undaunted, Joanne sent three sample chapters out to another agent, Christopher Little, whom she picked because she liked his name.

Her package landed on the desk of Bryony Evans, Christopher Little's office manager. She was intrigued by the story, although the agency did not normally handle children's books. Soon she asked Rowling to send in the rest of the manuscript. Rowling complied and Evans quickly read the entire book. She loved it. On her recommendation Christopher Little read the book, finishing it in one night, and the agency wrote back to Rowling within days. They offered to represent the manuscript and requested some minor revisions. Evans wanted Neville, a bumbling but kindhearted friend of Harry's, to play more of a role. Little wanted Joanne to explain Quidditch more thoroughly.

Joanne ranks receiving Little's letter as one of the high points of her life. After opening it, she read it eight times. According to Evans, Rowling wrote back and said, "That's brilliant because I like Neville, and, oh great, I can put the rules of Quidditch back in."

Still, Joanne knew that representation by an agent didn't guarantee a sale to a publisher. She would have to be patient. Plus, Little cautioned her not to expect much money. Children's books rarely earned their authors more than $3,000 to $4,000. That didn't bother Rowling. All she wanted was to be able to make ends meet so she could keep on writing.

It took months to find a publisher. The book received at least four rejections—Rowling herself doesn't remember how many there were—but Little told Joanne not to worry. He felt confident that someone would want her uniquely entertaining book. Finally, Little sent the book to Bloomsbury Publishing, a midsize publishing house. He had spoken to the head of the children's book department at a book fair, and he knew they were looking for something a bit different. Little believed that Harry Potter fit the bill.

Little's instinct proved right. Barry Cunningham, the editorial director of the children's book department, loved the manuscript when it arrived in June 1996. He wanted to impress the company's directors to gain their support for the book, so he handed it over to Rosamund de la Hey, the department's marketing manager. After reading it, she and her colleagues enthusiastically joined the quest to get Harry accepted. They made multiple copies of the manuscript, stuffed each one with Smarties candies, and tied ribbons around them. Then they delivered the packages to their superiors, in whose hands Harry's fate rested. It didn't take the directors long to decide. The next day Cunningham offered to buy the book for about $3,300. Joanne eagerly accepted. Finally, Harry Potter was going to be in print!

Finishing the first Harry Potter book had by no means gotten the writing bug out of Joanne's system. She knew that Harry's story would comprise seven volumes, and she had already started work on the next one, tentatively called *Harry Potter and the Half-Blood Prince.* In her first meeting with Barry Cunningham, over dinner, she asked him how he felt about sequels. Although he was impressed by the detail with which Joanne had mapped out the seven-volume series, he pointed out that the first book hadn't even been published yet. Joanne didn't want to wait for a commitment from Bloomsbury before starting work on the second book, but she knew that she needed financial support if she was going to continue writing. The $3,300 from Bloomsbury hadn't gone very far. She was flat broke again, barely able to make ends meet with the money she earned from teaching part-time. She thought an arts grant might be the solution, and she applied to the Scottish Arts Council in 1996. Her application received extremely high marks, and she was awarded a grant for £8,000, about $13,000, the largest grant the council had ever given to a children's book author. When she received the money in February 1997, she bought a computer, which greatly speeded her work on the second Harry Potter book.

Meanwhile, *Harry Potter and the Philosopher's Stone* was being edited and readied for publication. Although Bloomsbury was excited about the book, they felt they needed to be cautious, in case such a lengthy children's book couldn't find an audience. In July 1997, *Harry Potter and the Philosopher's Stone* was published with a print run of only 500 copies. Joanne's full name didn't appear on the books; instead, she was listed as J. K. Rowling. The marketing department feared that boys wouldn't want to read a book by a female author, so the company had printed only Rowling's initials to disguise her gender. Joanne, eager to please them, had even picked out a middle name to provide a middle initial. She chose Kathleen, after her favorite grandmother. The ploy seemed to work. Many of the book's early fans assumed the author was male. In fact, the first fan letter Rowling ever received began "Dear Sir."

As for now, it never even occurred to Joanne that she would ever receive fan letters. She was just thrilled to see her book in print. When she received her first copy, she carried it around with her all day. Seeing the book in bookstores was another high point of her life. "The first time I saw it in a bookshop I had this mad desire to sign it," she said in *Telling Tales*. "It was an extraordinary moment."

Harry Potter and the Philosopher's Stone *was published
with a print run of 500
copies. Positive reviews and
word of mouth created great
demand for the book, and
soon thousands more copies
were printed.*

The first review of the book appeared in the *Scotsman,*
Scotland's national newspaper. Happily, it was quite
positive, and it was soon followed by other complimentary reviews. This praise as well as word of mouth
created demand for the book, and soon Bloomsbury

had to print thousands more copies. Joanne felt that she had arrived. All her life she had dreamed of seeing a book she had written displayed on bookstore shelves. Now her life's ambition had finally been achieved. She had no idea that the saga of Harry Potter and Joanne "Kathleen" Rowling was just beginning.

*Rowling and her books created a frenzy, and not just at book signings like this one at Harrods department store. American publishers entered a fierce bidding war for the chance to publish* Harry Potter and the Philosopher's Stone *in the United States.*

# 5

# HARRY POTTER TAKES OFF

UNKNOWN TO JOANNE, the buzz created by Harry Potter had crossed the Atlantic, even before the book landed on bookstore shelves there. Arthur Levine, editorial director of Arthur A. Levine Books, an imprint of Scholastic Books, heard that Bloomsbury had an exciting new children's title. He obtained prepublication proofs of the book, and like everyone else, he immediately loved it. He knew he wanted to buy the American rights to the book.

He got his chance at the 1997 book fair in Bologna, Italy, about three months after the book had come out in Britain. Knowing there was interest, Christopher Little set up an auction for the rights. The bidding was fierce. Little called Joanne that night at 8:00 to tell her the auction was taking place and that the bid was up to five figures. "I went cold with shock," Joanne said in an interview published in *Salon* magazine.

Levine, convinced the book would be a hit, was determined to land it. The bidding climbed higher and higher, and at 10 P.M., Little called Rowling again. This time the bidding was up to six figures. Joanne could hardly believe it. About an hour later the auction was over, and Levine had agreed to pay $105,000 for the American rights to *Harry Potter and the Philosopher's Stone.* It was the highest sum ever paid for the rights to a foreign children's book. Levine immediately got on the phone and called Rowling, even though it was 11 P.M. in Britain. In an article in the *New York Times* he said, "My first reaction was to call the author, J. K. Rowling, to tell her not to be frightened because I knew it would be a tremendous amount of pressure on her."

Joanne was still in shock when her phone rang and Arthur Levine was on the line. "Don't be scared," he told her. "Thanks, I am," she replied. They had a short, pleasant conversation, and Levine urged her not to worry.

Despite Levine's kind words, Joanne couldn't sleep that night. "On one level I was obviously delighted," she told *Salon* magazine, "but most of me froze."

The unprecedented sum that Levine paid for Harry Potter generated a wave of media attention that nearly overwhelmed Joanne as she struggled to write the second book. She realized that she had a decision to make. Should she continue to teach and accept slow progress on Book Two? Or should she quit teaching and write full-time? She estimated that with the Scholastic windfall she could survive for at least two years, even if the Harry Potter phenomenon fizzled. She would be risking her teaching career, however, as it would mean leaving the profession for several years.

Joanne decided to go for it. After all, being a full-time writer had always been her dream. It proved to be a good decision, as *Harry Potter and the Philosopher's Stone* began winning awards. First was the Nestlé Smarties prize in November 1997, then the British Book Awards Children's Book of the Year in February 1998. As the prizes mounted, so did sales, and Joanne received her first royalty check. "That was a very proud moment," she said

in *Telling Tales*. Soon she moved out of her tiny apartment into a rented house in Edinburgh.

The Harry Potter phenomenon didn't even come close to fizzling. Soon the book climbed to the top of the best-seller lists in the United Kingdom. It was so popular among adults that Bloomsbury released a new version of the book with a more mature, understated cover so adult Harry fans wouldn't feel compelled to hide the book behind a newspaper while reading it on the train. The media attention continued to grow. Suddenly Joanne was giving newspaper and magazine interviews in Nicolson's Café, rather than writing there. It wasn't long before she became annoyed by

*The duke of Edinburgh greets J. K. Rowling at an awards event. Even members of the royal family profess an interest in the exploits of Harry Potter.*

the media's unrelenting emphasis on a chapter of her life she was trying to put behind her—the six months she had spent on public assistance. Publications everywhere latched on to her rags-to-riches story, depicting her as an example of a welfare mother making good. Her protestations that she was on assistance only briefly—and then only because of a lack of access to child care—went unnoticed, as did her middle-class upbringing and university degree.

Some articles even used her success to imply that other single mothers receiving assistance should be able to find gainful employment as fiction writers. Rowling found that infuriating. "That's absolute rubbish," she later said to a *Time* magazine reporter. "This is not vanity or arrogance, but if you look at the facts, very, very few people manage to write anything that might be a best seller. Therefore, I'm lucky by anyone's standards, let alone single mothers' standards."

With all the distractions, Joanne was suffering from writer's block as she worked on Book Two. "I was worried that it wouldn't live up to readers' expectations," she said in *Telling Tales*. Although she did make her deadline in the spring of 1998, she actually took the book back for further work after submitting it to Bloomsbury. It was six more weeks before she was satisfied with it. During the writing process she had decided to change the title from *Harry Potter and the Half-Blood Prince* to *Harry Potter and the Chamber of Secrets* because "unfortunately the story bore no relation whatsoever to the title by the time I finished," she admitted in a chat at BBC Online.

*Chamber of Secrets* begins in much the same way as *Sorcerer's Stone:* at 4 Privet Drive, the home of Harry's mundane Muggle relatives, the Dursleys. Luckily, Harry is rescued from his miserable summer vacation by his friend Ron Weasley. He gets to spend the last few weeks in the Weasleys' truly magical household, where travel is from fireplace to fireplace via Floo powder, a ghoul has taken up residence in the attic, the dishes clean themselves, and the garden is infested with gnomes. Not the Muggle, stone-statue kind of gnomes, of course, but pointy-toothed little creatures that can only be driven off by swinging them around your head by the ankles and hurling them out of the yard as if they were bipedal discuses. Clearly, Rowling spent a great deal of energy making sure the second book would be as wildly inventive as the first.

Once at school Harry settles into the routine of the Hogwarts school year—trying to learn how to turn beetles into buttons; practicing Quidditch; and having conflicts with both Professor Snape, the Potions Master who has it in for Harry, and Draco Malfoy, the spoiled school bully who also reserves a special hatred for Harry.

In *Chamber of Secrets,* Rowling begins to explore two important themes hinted at in the first book, themes she would later reemphasize in Book Four: fame and prejudice. To exemplify the first, she introduces the character of Gilderoy Lockhart, the pompous airbag of a Defense Against the Dark Arts professor who seems to have few concerns beyond oiling his publicity machine. To Harry's chagrin, Lockhart takes him under his wing, leading Harry to be accused of being a fame seeker himself. Harry even acquires a fan, Colin Creevey, a first-year Gryffindor who drives Harry crazy snapping his picture and requesting autographs.

The prejudice theme rears its ugly head when Draco Malfoy calls Hermione a Mudblood, the foulest possible name for a Muggle-born wizard. The story takes an even darker turn when several students are attacked and magical graffiti claims the mythical Chamber of Secrets—a hidden room supposedly containing a horror that will purge the school of all Muggle-born wizards—has been opened.

The book also continues to explore the theme of loneliness Rowling introduced in Book One. For much of the book Harry, always the first on each crime scene and the possessor of a strange power usually associated with Dark wizards, is shunned by his classmates, who believe him responsible for the attacks.

The book's requisite mystery is resolved in a similar fashion to that of Book One, with an exciting conclusion fraught with danger and sporting several clever plot twists. Readers obviously judged *Chamber of Secrets* a worthy successor to the popular first book. When Book Two came out in Britain in July 1998, it immediately vaulted to the top of the best-seller lists.

The release of *Chamber of Secrets* in Britain was followed a few months later by the highly anticipated release of the first book in the United States. The American version wasn't quite the same book, however. First of all, Levine—with Joanne's help—had changed the title to *Harry Potter and the Sorcerer's Stone,* worried that the original title would fail to excite American readers. He also had an editor Americanize some British spellings and words, such as changing *colour* to *color* and *jumper* to *sweater.* The layout of the book was changed as well. Small black-and-white thematic illustrations appeared at the beginning of each chapter, making the American version somewhat longer. The cover illustration and the interior drawings were created by artist Mary GrandPré, and Joanne was quite pleased by the artwork.

The changes attracted some criticism, and Scholastic was accused of "translating" the book to coddle American readers. Particularly offensive, said critics, were changes that altered the meaning of words, like changing *crumpet* to *English muffin.* Although both are breakfast foods, they aren't the same thing. Rowling found the criticism over-wrought: "Changes were only made when words meant something completely different in America. . . . The changes really were minimal."

Apparently most readers didn't care. *Harry Potter and the Sorcerer's Stone* soared to the top of the *New York Times* best-seller list shortly after its September 1998 release. The Harry Potter phenomenon—and Rowling's personal fortune—was growing faster than Joanne could ever have imagined. The first book was being translated

*The Harry Potter phenomenon knows no cultural or geographical bounds. Here a bookstore in Munich, Germany, displays advertisements for* Harry Potter und der Feuerkelch (Harry Potter and the Goblet of Fire).

into more than 20 different languages. In the United States and Britain the books were outselling perennially popular adult authors like John Grisham and Tom Clancy. Rowling had a contract in hand from Bloomsbury to produce the remaining five Harry Potter books. Plus, in October 1998 Joanne and her agent sold the movie rights to the Harry Potter series to Warner Brothers for a reported $2 million.

At first Joanne had been reluctant to sell the movie

rights, despite offers from several studios, because she was worried that no one would tell Harry's story properly. Eventually, however, she became convinced that Warner Brothers would do a good job, based on their adaptations of the children's classics *The Secret Garden* and *The Little Princess*. Once she'd made the decision, she started looking forward to seeing the film. "I can't wait to see how they will pull off a Quidditch game," she said in a chat published in the *Boston Globe.*

With the publication of Book Two in Britain a year before its scheduled release in the United States, Harry Potter began to run afoul of international copyright law—a more serious violation than sneaking around Hogwarts after curfew. Eager Americans, unable to stand the long wait for the American version of *Harry Potter and the Chamber of Secrets,* began ordering the book through online booksellers, like Amazon.com's British subsidiary, Amazon.co.uk. Scholastic Press and Christopher Little protested this flow of contraband Harry Potter, pointing out that Scholastic had paid for the right to publish the book in the United States. Every Bloomsbury-printed book that sneaked across the Atlantic represented lost sales for Scholastic. However, Amazon did nothing to stop the practice. Officially, international copyright law allows the export of one book per customer as long as it is for personal use only.

Meanwhile, after carefully plotting out the five books remaining in the series, Joanne was hard at work on Book Three, *Harry Potter and the Prisoner of Azkaban.* By now, she understood what it meant to be famous. She could no longer write at Nicolson's; fans and journalists were seeking her out there. She found it ironic that now that she was a full-time writer, she had less time to write than ever. Publicity duties, such as interviews and book signings, dominated her schedule. Still, she managed to finish Book Three in record time, taking only a year to write it.

According to Rowling, she had been looking forward to writing the third book of the series ever since the first months of developing Harry's world. She couldn't wait to write about Professor Lupin, a shabbily dressed, frail-looking man who becomes Harry's third professor of Defense Against the Dark Arts in three years. He and the secrets he hides are a hugely important part of the book's plot.

As always, the book begins at the Dursleys' home. Harry doesn't stay long, however. When Uncle Vernon's aggressively nasty sister, Aunt Marge, insults Harry's parents, Harry loses control of his temper—and his magic. (Marge, a dog lover, is based somewhat on Rowling's maternal grandmother, Frieda, who, as Rowling said in *Telling Tales*, "was obsessed with dogs, which she much preferred to humans.") Harry ends up fleeing the house with his belongings. Just as he is wondering where to go, Rowling adds a humorous new twist to her wizarding world: the Knight Bus, "emergency transport for the stranded witch or wizard." The conductor and driver of the bus, which appears out of nowhere to pick up Harry, are named Stan and Ernie, after Rowling's grandfathers. Stan and Ernie transport Harry to Diagon Alley, the hidden wizard enclave in London, where he stays for the remaining weeks of the summer. Harry's eager anticipation of the start of the school year is spoiled when he finds out that not only has Sirius Black, a dangerous Dark wizard convicted of murdering 13 people, escaped from the wizard prison, Azkaban, but he's now after Harry.

On the train ride to Hogwarts, Harry has his first encounter with Azkaban's sinister prison guards, the dementors. When confronted by one, Harry faints amid a feeling of dread and begins recalling the terrible moment when Voldemort murdered his parents. As the book progresses, Harry has several more encounters with the dementors, and each time he remembers more about his parents' death. *Prisoner of Azkaban* is the first book in which Rowling delves into Harry's past, making the reader feel the horror of what happened to Harry's family. When Harry asks why he is more sensitive to the dementors than anyone else, Professor Lupin replies, "The dementors affect you worse than the others because there are horrors in your past that the others don't have."

Rowling uses the dementors to explore fear and hopelessness, drawing on her experience with depression during her time on public assistance. Another important theme, explored further in Book Four, is that of conflicts between friends, so typical of young adolescents. Ron and Hermione get into a long-running feud after Hermione's cat, Crookshanks, appears to have eaten Ron's pet rat, Scabbers. Later, the theme of loneliness reappears when Hagrid tries to repair the damage by lecturing Ron and Harry, "[Hermione's] bin comin' down ter visit me a lot since Chris'mas. Bin feelin' lonely. . . . She's cried a fair few times, yeh know."

As with her two other books, Rowling crafts an energetic plot that drives to a stunning conclusion—with a lot of twists and turns along the way. In the process readers find out a wealth of information about Harry's past, revealing the importance of the small details Rowling planted into the earlier volumes, as far back as the first chapter of Book One.

Bloomsbury knew they were going to have another hit on their hands. They carefully timed the British release of *Harry Potter and the Prisoner of Azkaban* to take place at 3:45 P.M. on July 8, 1999, right at the end of the school day. The ploy worked wonderfully. Children went straight from school to stand in line at their nearest bookstore. A mere two weeks after its release, the book had gone through 10 printings, selling 270,000 copies.

A month before, in June 1999, Scholastic had finally released Book Two, *Harry Potter and the Chamber of*

*Secrets,* in the United States. Finally the company could breathe a sigh of relief, lean back, and begin counting its profits. Unfortunately, though, as soon as *Prisoner of Azkaban* hit bookstores in Britain, Scholastic once again had to endure thousands of British copies of the latest Harry Potter book being shipped across the Atlantic to eager American fans. Trying to minimize the problem, the company narrowed the gap between the releases of Books Two and Three, waiting only a few months before releasing the American version of *Harry Potter and the Prisoner of Azkaban* on September 7, 1999. Next time there would be no opportunity for Amazon.co.uk to make a mint on violating Scholastic's territorial rights. Bloomsbury and Scholastic, along with the Canadian publisher, Raincoast Books, were already planning to release Book Four simultaneously.

Only days after its release in the United States, *Harry Potter and the Prisoner of Azkaban* had grabbed the top spot on the *New York Times* best-seller list—followed by the two other Harry Potter books, at spots two and three. This dominance of the list by a teenage wizard began to irritate some American publishers of adult fiction. Rumblings began that some publishers were going to ask the *Times* to remove the Harry Potter titles from the regular fiction list, arguing that as children's books, they had never belonged there anyway.

Joanne hardly had time to worry about copyright and best-seller list controversies. After all, her fans were already clamoring for Book Four. Her deadline was spring 2000, and she knew that the book would be a crucial turning point for Harry—and the longest volume to date.

*After publishing her third book, J. K. Rowling wasn't just a famous author, she was also rich. Her net worth was £14.5 million ($20 million) by the fall of 1999.*

# 6

# *THE GOBLET OF FIRE* AND BEYOND

BY THIS POINT Joanne wasn't just famous. She was also rich. Her net worth, around £14.5 million ($20 million) by the fall of 1999, stood to grow considerably after she and agent Christopher Little finalized a deal to sell merchandising rights to Warner Brothers. Unfortunately, the downside to her fame and fortune was the constant public attention. She had to put up with fans and journalists watching her house, which was right on the street in downtown Edinburgh, and knocking on her door at all hours. In addition, the fan mail was taking over the house.

It was time to move. Joanne bought a larger, more private house in Edinburgh and hired a full-time secretary to help with the fan mail. She still, however, continued to write in cafés, although she had to give up her beloved Nicolson's to avoid being interrupted by fans and journalists. She still continued to walk around Edinburgh, or hire a driver, because she didn't own a car. There was a simple reason for this lack of something she could now easily afford: she had never learned how to drive!

71

In October 1999, Joanne went on a three-week book tour to promote *Harry Potter and the Prisoner of Azkaban* in the United States. Not, of course, that the book really needed promoting. She described the tour, which began in Boston, in *Telling Tales:* "As we were driving up to the bookshop I saw a massive queue snaking along two blocks. I asked Kris, from the publisher, Scholastic, if there was a sale on and she told me the queue was for me. It was the most extraordinary experience. . . . I signed 1,400 books that day." Although Joanne enjoyed talking to her fans— "Meeting kids who've read the books is pure, unadulterated pleasure," she said in a *USA Today* article—she was distressed that many had to go home disappointed when lines for book signings proved to be too long. Throughout the eight-city tour she drew at least 1,000 fans at every appearance, signing more than 40,000 books at the 31 bookstores she visited.

Her favorite cities in the United States were New York and San Francisco. An art enthusiast, she was disappointed that she couldn't find the time to visit any of New York's art galleries. She did, however, succeed in visiting the Kennedy Museum while she was in Boston, indulging a personal fascination with the famous American political family. Six-year-old Jessica, who accompanied her mother on tour, had more opportunities for sightseeing than Joanne did. For months after the tour she kept gloating that she had gotten to go up in Seattle's Space Needle and her mom hadn't.

After she returned to Scotland, Rowling settled back into writing. She found Book Four, rumored to be titled *Harry Potter and the Doomspell Tournament,* difficult to write, and she struggled with its darker tone, its crucial plot, and the onset of puberty for Harry and his friends. One particular stumbling block was chapter 9, a pivotal chapter in which an ugly event at the Quidditch World Cup makes it clear that the evil Voldemort still has supporters in the wizarding world. She wrote 13 different versions of the chapter before she finally came up with one she could stand. She later discussed her struggle during an online chat at Comicrelief.com: "At one point, I thought of missing it out altogether and just putting in a page saying 'Chapter Nine was too difficult' and going straight to Chapter Ten." Matters took a turn for the worse when she realized there was a significant flaw in the plot. It took Joanne nearly three months of rewriting to fix it. During this time she refused all interviews and did no publicity appearances so she could have maximum writing time. She kept up a strenuous pace of 10- to 12-hour days to try to stay on schedule.

On one particularly bad day Rowling spent hours in her favorite café staring at a blank piece of paper. She couldn't get her mind off the exaggerated story of her marriage that had recently appeared in a newspaper, courtesy of her ex-husband. Suddenly, she gave herself a mental kick, reminding herself that fame had a definite upside—money. That's when she made the only extravagant purchase of her life. She marched down to a jewelry store on Prince Street and dropped thousands of dollars on a huge aquamarine ring. She calls it her "No One Is Grinding Me Down Ring" and laughingly describes it as "obscene . . . You can't type with it because it's so heavy." She bought gifts for two friends as well. The purchases improved her mood—which was exactly the point.

Finally, in spring 2000, Joanne finished the book. With the manuscript in editing, Joanne had time to give a 90-minute press conference in London, and she participated in several online chats. Readers were eager to hear what Book Four might have in store for them. Unfortunately, Rowling revealed little information, even withholding the book's title. The tidbits she revealed were: Harry, Hermione, and Ron begin to notice the opposite sex; a significant character dies; Harry goes to the Quidditch World Cup; and students from other wizardry schools make an appearance.

*Queen Elizabeth II of England (left), a fan of Harry Potter, visits with Rowling and her editor Emma Matthewson during "Themed Books Day" in London.*

In June, Rowling was honored to discover that Harry Potter was popular among the royal family as well. The queen announced that Rowling would be awarded the title Officer of the Order of the British Empire, usually called OBE. The awards ceremony would take place the following spring.

Finally, on July 8, 2000, came the moment every Harry Potter fan was waiting for: the release of Book Four—entitled *Harry Potter and the Goblet of Fire*—at the peak of a carefully orchestrated Harry Potter frenzy.

Right from the beginning of *Goblet of Fire* the reader knows that this book will be different from the other three. For the first time Rowling strays from her opening-chapter formula. Rather than beginning with humorous events at the Dursleys', Rowling starts the book with a creepy, serious chapter involving Lord Voldemort that reads more like a horror novel than lighthearted fare about a boy wizard.

After that scene the book settles back into a more comfortable pattern, as if awaking from a nightmare—which Harry, incidentally, does. Once again, Harry is suffering in his miserable life with the Dursleys during summer vacation. Luckily, Ron saves Harry again, and this time his father has tickets to the Quidditch World Cup. Rowling's satirical bent is quite in evidence in her description of the World Cup; the match is a humorous spoof of real-world sporting events, complete with a brawl between competing mascots, numerous fouls on the field, and a dramatic finish.

Chapter 9, however, which takes place shortly after the World Cup game ends, is another indication that Rowling intends for the series to become darker in tone. Here, in this chapter she had so much difficulty writing, she revisits the theme of prejudice that she touched on in *Chamber of Secrets*. In the middle of the night a masked group of wizards marches through the campsite, torturing a help-less family of Muggles. The scene is very reminiscent of a Ku Klux Klan lynching.

After the World Cup, Harry finally gets to Hogwarts—which isn't until chapter 12—but Rowling still isn't finished lobbing curveballs. This school year will be different; instead of the interhouse Quidditch competition, Hogwarts will be hosting the Triwizard Tournament, a competition between wizarding schools that hasn't been held for hun-dreds of years. *Goblet of Fire* is the first book to mention the existence of other wizardry schools.

Despite these changes, Hogwarts is still quite familiar, with tough classes and homework in plenty. And Rowling continues to sprinkle humor throughout, aided by her understated style: "Just then, Neville caused a slight diver-sion by turning into a large canary." Or take her description of Harry's pathetic Christmas present from the Dursleys—it "consisted of a single tissue, an all-time low."

Although humor is present, of course, Book Four is unquestionably a much more serious book than any of the previous ones. Rowling revisits many of the themes she touched on in *Chamber of Secrets*, such as loneliness and Harry's frustration with his fame. In fact, here they are linked. When Harry ends up competing in the Triwizard Tournament, Ron's jealousy over Harry's fame finally gets the better of him. Again, as in Book Two, Harry finds that most of the school is angry with him. But this time Ron is among them. "The next few days were some of Harry's worst at Hogwarts. . . . He thought he could have coped with the rest of the school's behavior if he could just have had Ron back as a friend. . . . It was lonely with dislike pouring in on him from all sides."

Ron's anger with Harry is exacerbated by the press attention Harry receives. In this book Rowling introduces Rita Skeeter, an annoying journalist who loves to fabricate stories to embarrass people. Although Rowling has been accused of creating Rita in response to the heavy-handed treatment her personal story received in the press, that's not the case. "The fact is, Rita was planned all along," she told Lizo of BBC Online. She did admit, however, that her battles with the press made writing Rita even more enjoyable.

Although Ron and Harry patch up their differences, it's not the end of Rowling's theme of conflict among friends. This time it's the onset of puberty that causes friction—between Ron and Hermione. When Hermione goes to the Christmas Ball with someone else, Ron is jealous, although he won't admit it.

By the end, however, the three friends are getting along again, and Rowling once more crafts a dramatic ending with multiple plot twists. As promised, a character dies, and the story takes a much darker turn as it becomes clear that evil has taken a firm hold on Harry's lighthearted world. This is the first book in which Rowling directly explores the theme of death by allowing Harry to witness the demise of another character, a death in which Voldemort is involved. In an article in the October 30, 2000, issue of *Time* magazine Rowling discussed why she felt the death was necessary: "If you're choosing to write about evil, you really do have a moral obligation to show what that means . . . [Voldemort] . . . is incredibly power hungry.

Racist, really. And what do those kinds of people do? They treat human life so lightly." Although she knew the death was necessary, Rowling didn't find the ending easy to write. "I actually cried twice during the ending of Book Four," she said.

Despite the change in tone, Book Four set publishing records with its rapid sales. Not long after kids and parents stood in line at midnight on July 8 to get *Goblet of Fire,* and the Hogwarts Express pulled out of London's King's Cross Station, the *New York Times* bowed to pressure from numerous publishing houses and created a new best-seller list strictly for children's books. The paper stated that the list was conceived to acknowledge the increased popularity of children's books. Regardless of the reason for the list's creation, the result was that Harry Potter was unceremoniously banished from the list just in time to prevent all four of his books from holding the top four spots. Instead, they grabbed the top four slots on the newly

*Thousands of people around the world—like these fans in Omaha, Nebraska—waited in line for a chance to purchase a copy of* Harry Potter and the Goblet of Fire, *which was released at midnight on July 8, 2000.*

created children's best-seller list. The list was later divided into paperbacks, picture books, and chapter books. As of May 2001, Harry Potter still held four of the top six slots on the children's chapter book list.

Initially, Rowling hadn't planned to read any of the books to Jessica until she was seven years old. But she had already broken that promise. With Jessica being badgered by older classmates for insider secrets and continually asking other children about the terms she was hearing in the schoolyard, like "Quidditch" and "Hogwarts," Joanne relented. Luckily, Jessica took the books in stride; in fact, she became quite a Harry Potter fan. But Rowling was worried that Book Four, which contained a death, would be too much for her young daughter. She needn't have worried. "She wasn't scared at all," Rowling wrote in an online chat at Barnesandnoble.com. "As long as Harry was okay, she didn't seem to care."

In October 2000, Rowling went on another tour to North America, but this time she didn't visit the United States. Instead she flew to its neighbor to the north, Canada. On October 22 she read from her books to a rapt audience of more than 10,000 people, mostly children, in Toronto's SkyDome. It was the biggest crowd ever to hear an author read his or her work.

Rowling is willing not only to spend time with her fans, but to donate her time and energy to worthy causes. In October 2000 she agreed to become involved in a cause close to her heart: championing the rights of single mothers. She became the spokeswoman for a British charity, the National Council for One Parent Families, and donated $725,000 to the organization. In her first speech as the organization's ambassador, on December 5, 2000, she criticized several government officials, such as Anne Widdecombe, a leading conservative politician, and John Major, the former prime minister, for previous comments they had made. Both officials stated that two-parent families were the norm and implied that single-parent

families were undesirable and inferior. Rowling argued that the biggest obstacle for the children of single parents was poverty, not the lack of a second parent.

The National Council for One Parent Families is not the only recipient of Rowling's largesse. In April 2001 she announced her intention to assist Scotland's multiple sclerosis society in her mother's memory. But the charitable activity that meant the most to Harry Potter fans was the release in March 2001 of two tiny books based on fictitious Hogwarts schoolbooks. Rowling donated all proceeds from the books' sales to Comic Relief, a British charity devoted to helping children in the developing world. The short paperbacks, entitled *Quidditch Through the Ages* and *Fantastic Beasts and Where to Find Them*, were "ghostwritten" by Rowling under the names Kennilworthy Whisp and Newt Scamander. The books offered an opportunity for Rowling to showcase her remarkable

*Remembering John Major's hurtful remarks about single mothers, Rowling gives her time and money to charity organizations like the National Council for One Parent Families.*

imagination and sense of humor. *Fantastic Beasts* is a "duplicate" of Harry Potter's personal copy of the book, so it features amusing handwritten comments by the boy wizard and his friends Ron and Hermione, as well as sketches drawn by Rowling herself. *Quidditch Through the Ages* is meant to represent a popular library book, so it lacks handwritten marginal comments, although it, too, features several Rowling sketches. The carefully described history of Quidditch in *Quidditch Through the Ages* is hilarious, including cleverly devised "source" material such as this 14th-century poem by Ingolf the Iambic:

> Oh the thrill of the chase as I soar through the air
> With the Snitch up ahead and the wind in my hair
> As I draw ever closer, the crowd gives a shout
> But then comes a Bludger and I am knocked out.

The two books sold well, snapped up by Harry Potter fans eager for a morsel of Rowling's magic while awaiting Book Five. In fact, a week before they were released, preorders from excited fans had made the pair of books, sold as a set, the number two item on Amazon.com. They were still selling well months after publication, helped by rave reviews from fans who appreciated the attention to detail in the small volumes, from the claw marks on the cover of *Fantastic Beasts* to the prices on both books listed in Sickles and Knuts to the amusing forewords and back-cover copy attributed to Albus Dumbledore, Hogwarts's headmaster. The back of *Fantastic Beasts* offers a warning to ungenerous Muggles: "If you feel that [Comic Relief] is insufficient reason to part with your money, I can only hope most sincerely that passing wizards feel more charitable if they ever see you being attacked by a Manticore." And in *Quidditch,* Dumbledore warns of possible repercussions from mishandling the library book: "Though I have removed the usual library book spells from this volume, I cannot promise that every trace has gone. . . . I myself doodled absentmindedly on a copy of *Theories of Transubstantial Transfiguration* last year and next moment found the book beating me fiercely about the head."

Perhaps writing these amusing volumes was an enjoyable break for Rowling after the stress of writing *Goblet of Fire*. She also took time out to write the final chapter of the seventh book. She expects to have to rewrite it when she composes Book Seven, but she says having a rough draft of the chapter gives her faith that she will get to the end of the series, eventually.

In the meantime, Rowling had to get to work on Book Five. At first Scholastic and Bloomsbury claimed the fifth book would be out in summer 2001. By November 2000, however, agent Christopher Little announced that the date had been pushed back indefinitely, probably until 2002. Rowling was unwilling to commit to the exhausting 10-hour days she had endured while working on Book Four, which had left her close to a nervous breakdown. But she did release a little information about the next installment: it will be called *Harry Potter and the Order of the Phoenix,* it will explain why Harry has to return to the Dursleys' every summer, Ginny Weasley will play more of a role, and readers will find out where Percy Weasley's loyalties lie. In addition, some previous characters will make a reappearance, particularly Professor Lupin from Book Three, and there will finally be a female professor of Defense Against the Dark Arts.

The ending of Book Four also hints at what is to come. A major conflict with Voldemort looms on the horizon, and *Order of the Phoenix* is almost certain to continue the darker tone Rowling established in *Goblet of Fire*. Still, near the end of the book Rowling suggests that her particular brand of humor will be present no matter how dark the plots of the books may get. Harry, speaking to Fred and George Weasley—notorious pranksters—says, "We could all do with a few laughs. I've got a feeling we're going to need them more than usual before long."

*At the dawn of the 21st century children weren't reading and parents were concerned. Harry Potter helped change that. This youngster breakfasts with J. K. Rowling after winning a Harry Potter essay contest.*

# 7

# A LITERARY PHENOMENON

AS THE 21ST century approached, school librarians, parents, and teachers shared a major worry about American children: they weren't reading. With television, video games, and the Internet providing constant distraction and temptation, modern kids simply couldn't be induced to spend time curled up with a book.

Yet suddenly, with the American release of *Harry Potter and the Sorcerer's Stone* in September 1998, all bets were off. As Harry's popularity grew, adults became accustomed to watching children lugging around the 309-page hardback and debating the finer points of the plot. Teachers, hoping to harness their enthusiasm, began reading the Potter books aloud in class and using passages from the books for grammar exercises.

What makes the books so popular? Kids seem to identify with the characters and, while also enjoying the books as an escape, seem to associate them with their own lives. In an interview quoted in the December 25, 2000, issue of *Time* magazine, one 12-year-old

Chicago native said, "The characters really relate to you—they're kids. They have bullies and bad teachers. It's helped me understand . . . people, maybe my friends, my teachers. It's influenced me to read more." Children who are living through difficult times—for example, battling illness—have found inspiration in Harry's determination to fight against difficult odds. Some adults have found similar inspiration in the books: best-selling horror writer Stephen King told Rowling that the books helped him get through his arduous recovery from a car accident in June 1999 that left him with a broken right hip and leg and a collapsed lung.

The Harry Potter mystique is particularly remarkable for its appeal to boys. ~~Girls generally read much more than boys~~, who rarely opt for the printed page outside of the Hardy Boys books in the 1970s and the Goosebumps series in the 1990s. In July 1999 the *New York Times* surveyed overnight camps for kids ages 8 to 15 around the United States. They found that the Harry Potter books were being widely read by both genders; in fact, about a third of the campers had already read them.

Happily, the phenomenon hasn't been confined to Harry Potter books. Once kids exhausted the available novels about the boy wizard, they began looking for substitutes. By 1999 publishers were seeing sales of other perennial children's favorites—as well as newer fantasy titles—skyrocket. They even coined a nickname for the phenomenon: the Harry Potter halo effect. The Chronicles of Narnia, C. S. Lewis's seven-volume series of books about British children's interactions with the magical world of Narnia, was on a pace to double its usual sales of 1.7 million volumes. Lloyd Alexander's five-volume Prydain series, which includes the well-known book *The Black Cauldron,* found its sales tripled. Kids also snapped up titles that J. K. Rowling cited as old favorites, such as *I Capture the Castle,* by Dodie

Smith, which enjoyed a fourfold increase in sales. In spring 2000, before *Harry Potter and the Goblet of Fire* arrived with fanfare at British and American bookstores, booksellers set up Harry Potter Withdrawal Clubs to cope with requests for reading recommendations. The American Booksellers Association, an association for independent booksellers, even created a top-ten list of

*Children of all ages are reading about Harry Potter. This five-year-old boy is begging his nine-year-old brother to read the fourth Harry Potter book to him. The five-year-old is also sporting Harry Potter–style glasses.*

books to recommend to Potter-starved fans. And to the delight of the publishing industry, young readers and their parents were now buying hardcover children's fiction instead of paperbacks, improving profits for publishers and bookstores alike.

Not everyone is thrilled with Harry's popularity, however, or views the books as the cure for American's lack of literacy. Many parents, convinced the books are immoral, have made headlines with their crusades to have the books made off-limits in classrooms and libraries. In southeastern Pennsylvania one father demanded that the books be removed from the curriculum because they encourage lying, stealing, cheating, and other moral failures. He cited examples such as Harry and Ron cheating on their Divination homework, Ron's mischievous older brothers stealing food from the kitchens, and Harry lying to his friend Hagrid, Hogwarts's giant-size groundskeeper.

Most opponents of the books have explicitly Christian reasons for wanting the books banned or at least removed from schools. Citing Scripture that warns against tolerating witchcraft, several groups and individuals have denounced the books as satanic because they contain wizards and witches. The fact that Harry and his friends are fighting for good against evil does not mollify such critics; they believe that the books are an evil influence because of their magical content, regardless of what the magic is used for. The American Library Association said that as of spring 2001 the Potter books had been challenged in school districts in 26 states. Some school districts have even pulled the books off library shelves. An article on the Christian news website Worthynews.com proclaimed that the Harry Potter books were leading children into paganism: "The fact is . . . many children are pursuing the real-life versions of witchcraft because they have learned to love Harry's world." The article's author, Berit Kjos, moves into his conclusion with:

"Remember, this is spiritual warfare. God's enemy fights as hard as ever to win the hearts and loyalties of our children."

However, these views don't represent those of all Christians. A search on Harry Potter and Christianity on the Web turns up numerous websites featuring articles by Christian groups who support the books, some who advise a cautious approach, and others who call them the work of Satan and caution that Harry Potter's lightning bolt scar is actually a mark of the devil. There have been several books written on the subject as well—some that are strongly opposed to Harry Potter, others that offer advice to Christian parents on how to discuss the books with their children.

Rowling is baffled by the flap over her books in the United States. She points out that Harry and his friends are clearly fighting against evil, not promoting it. "These books are fundamentally moral," she said in an online chat at Barnesandnoble.com. In the October 18, 1999, edition of the *Boston Globe* she said, "Harry can only get to a certain point in an adventure by breaking some rules. His particular role in the group is conscience. He will break the rule if he thinks he's doing it for the greater good. But he has a fundamental sense of honor."

On the subject of magic she said in *USA Today,* "I truly am bemused that anyone who has read the books could think that I am a proponent of the occult in any serious way." She pointed out that the majority of children's books include magic. "Magic is going to be a theme of children's literature as long as the human race exists." In reality, Rowling says, she doesn't believe in the sort of magic she depicts in her books. Although she agrees that parents have a right to control what their own children read, she finds attempts to censor the books offensive. "I am vehemently opposed to that," she added.

A perusal of the canon of children's literature supports Rowling's point. Magic and fantasy worlds have long

*Some parents believe Harry Potter promotes lying, stealing, and worship of the devil. This librarian holds up a certificate that he used to award children who successfully completed Book Four; the award was retired after parental complaints.*

been a staple of children's literature, from *Grimm's Fairy Tales* to Lewis Carroll's *Alice's Adventures in Wonderland* to the Christian-based Chronicles of Narnia series. Most children's fantasy books contain similar elements: the children are whisked off to a fantasy world, as in the Chronicles of Narnia, *Alice's Adventures in Wonderland,* and the *Wonderful Wizard of Oz,* by L. Frank Baum; a child discovers he has unsuspected magical powers, as in *The Dark Is Rising* by Susan Cooper; or the books are pure fantasy, set in a world where magic is part of the fabric of reality, as in *The Black Cauldron,* J. R. R. Tolkien's *The Hobbit,* and Ursula Le Guin's *A Wizard of Earthsea.* Often stories combine these elements. For example, in *A Wrinkle in Time,* by Madeleine L'Engle—a devoutly Christian writer—Meg's brother Charles is gifted with nearly superhuman intelligence, and Charles, Meg, and her friend Calvin take a trip with a trio of kindly witches to some very strange and frightening worlds. Yet nearly all critics have acclaimed these books.

It is true that Harry and his friends do behave immorally from time to time, particularly in the way they sneak around and lie to adults. This, too, however, is a time-honored tradition in children's literature. The reason, of course, is that if the children handed the solving of the book's mystery or crisis over to the adult characters, they would have nothing left to do but diligently work on their homework. And that wouldn't be very compelling reading. Writing for Salon.com, critic Charles Taylor points out that great children's novels have always emphasized the story over explicit moral teaching—otherwise, kids just don't read them: "Kids' lit can contain lessons, meanings, messages of comfort or heralds of experiences that lie in wait for young readers. But the minute any of those things overtakes narrative, the book is sunk."

In a multientry E-mail discussion of the Harry Potter books posted at Slate.msn.com, critics Polly Shulman and Tony Scott theorized about the popularity of the books among adults. They noted that the books bring adult readers back to a time of childhood sneak reading, hiding under the covers with a flashlight. The realistic moral ambiguity of the books, as well as their near absence of moral preaching, is also a draw for adults; although adults gleefully give children books rife with overt moralizing, they can't stand it themselves. The series draws a clear line between great good and great evil, but Rowling understands that daily life is full of small moral challenges that her realistically flawed characters won't always pass.

The books have been criticized for other shortcomings besides moral failure, of course. An article by Christine Schoefer on Salon.com pointed out that the books are quite sexist. Hermione is the only strong female character in the books, and she is often portrayed as an annoying, bookish know-it-all who crumbles to tears under pressure. Schoefer has a point; most of the characters with a major impact on the plots of the books—Harry, Ron, Professor Dumbledore, Hagrid, Professor Snape—are male. On the other hand, Hogwarts is strictly coed, with integrated houses (although boys and girls have separate rooms) and Quidditch teams. The lack of strong female characters doesn't seem to hinder the books' popularity among girls or women. Schoefer admits she enjoyed the books, as did her three daughters. Rowling thinks feminist criticism of her books is exaggerated, and she believes that Hermione is quite a strong character. She has mentioned, however, that about six months into writing the first book, she suddenly wondered why she hadn't made Harry a girl character. "But it was too late," she said, "Harry was too real for me to change. And I liked him too much by that time."

Other criticism comes from well-known literary critics, some of whom branded the books mere fluff. In an article in the *London Observer,* British critic Anthony Holden called them "one-dimensional children's books, Disney cartoons written in words, no more." Another *Observer* critic, Robert McCrum, wrote, "Her prose is as flat (and as English) as old beer." Harold Bloom, Sterling Professor of Humanities at Yale University, wrote in the *Wall Street Journal,* "Her prose style, heavy on clichés, makes no demands upon her readers." Luckily for Rowling, readers overwhelmingly tend to choose books that make no demands upon them and provide enjoyable escapes from reality. Not all critics have blasted the books, of course. Most reviews have been favorable, and the books have garnered numerous literary prizes, winning the Smarties

*Rowling holds her Order of the British Empire (OBE) award, which she received on March 2, 2001. She has also won many other prestigious awards, including the Children's Book of the Year.*

Gold Award three years in a row, two consecutive Children's Book of the Year Awards, and two Author of the Year Awards from the Booksellers' Association, to name a few.

Charles Taylor is firmly in the camp that believes Rowling's books deserve to be called children's classics. "I don't think you can read 100 pages of *Harry Potter and the Sorcerer's Stone* before you start feeling that unmistakable shiver that tells you you're reading a classic," he wrote in an article for Salon.com. He found *Sorcerer's Stone* to be a delightful, wonderfully written tale that speaks to kids' desire to belong as well as their sense of humor. He compares the books favorably with those of Roald Dahl, author of *James and the Giant Peach* and *Charlie and the Chocolate Factory,* writing, "*Harry Potter and the Sorcerer's Stone* unites the English novel of school day exploits with the humorous, macabre fantasy that Dahl perfected."

In the November 20, 1999, issue of the *New York Times,* critic Richard Bernstein theorized that the popularity of the Harry Potter books among children may stem from their similarity to traditional fairy tales. In the 1970s a child psychologist named Bruno Bettelheim published a study of children's literature in which he found fairy tales to be of significant psychological power. He explained that the dark nature of the tales give voice to the terrors that children experience, with the usual happy ending sending the message that those fears can be overcome. The Potter books have many elements of the fairy tale, particularly the beginning of the story, when Harry is living with the Dursleys. Like Cinderella, Harry lives with evil stepparents (or in this case, an aunt and uncle), is picked on by his "siblings" (his cousin Dudley), and is treated shamefully, living in a closet under the stairs and receiving few clothes and poor food. Yet he overcomes these atrocious beginnings—as well as bullying classmates and teachers at school—to discover himself as brave, even heroic.

Rowling herself understands that casting Harry as an orphan was a nod to literary tradition. "All through literature—and not just children's—the hero has been removed from the family setting. . . . It serves the important function of enabling the hero to act without the fear of destroying his family and disappointing people who love him, or . . . having to expect frailties in his parents. I think that it serves an important function for readers, particularly child readers, to be able to explore adult cruelty, whether or not they are experiencing it themselves."

The Harry Potter books are such a tremendous success

precisely because, despite their fantasy world, they depict children as they actually are, not as they ought to be. Like the average American—or British—kid, Harry Potter isn't perfect, nor are his friends. Sometimes they lie, or are cruel to one another, or hide the truth from adults. But their hearts are in the right place, and they always choose the greater good over pettiness or selfishness. If Harry Potter, rather than confronting the evil Voldemort himself, had reported his suspicions of wrongdoing to headmaster Albus Dumbledore, then cheerfully devoted himself to his studies, J. K. Rowling would still be a French teacher and no one would ever have heard of the bespectacled boy wizard.

*A scene from the motion picture* Harry Potter and the Sorcerer's Stone, *released in November of 2001. Rowling strove to make certain that the movie was true to the book and that Harry didn't become merchandized to death.*

# 8

# HARRY POTTER
# AND THE
# MEDIA EMPIRE

THE WORLD OF Harry Potter no longer exclusively belongs to J. K. Rowling. Everyone who has read the books feels as if a piece of the world belongs to them. Rowling doesn't mind that some of her fans feel that way; according to an interview posted on Scholastic's website, one of her favorite fan comments came from a 12-year-old Scottish girl she met at a crowded book signing. The girl said, "I didn't WANT there to be so many people here, because this is MY book!" Unfortunately, that girl has to share Harry Potter not only with millions of other fans, but also with corporate America, which owns the lion's share of Harry's rights.

The first step toward Harry Potter's mass marketing took place when Rowling and her agent sold the movie rights to *Harry Potter and the Sorcerer's Stone* to Warner Brothers in October 1998. Joanne made certain that she would retain some input on the production, winning the right to review the screenplay and insisting that the film be live action, not animated. After rumors flew for months about who would direct the movie, Warner Brothers settled on Chris Columbus, director of *Mrs. Doubtfire* and *Home Alone.* Nervous fans worried it was a sign that the film would be thoroughly American and Hollywood. Thankfully, Warner Brothers bowed to Rowling's wishes that the film be wholly British, and they cast young, inexperienced British actors Daniel Radcliffe, Emma Watson, and Rupert Grint as Harry, Hermione, and Ron. The rest of the cast was British as well, including John Cleese (of Monty Python fame) as the ghost Nearly Headless Nick, Richard Harris (*Camelot, Unforgiven, Gladiator*) as Professor Dumbledore, and Alan Rickman (*Sense and Sensibility, Die Hard)* as Professor Snape, to name a few. The movie was filmed at Leavesden Studios in Hertfordshire—the same studio where the bulk of *Star Wars* was filmed—as well as on location at Hogwarts, better known as Gloucester Cathedral. Award-winning composer John Williams, of *Star Wars* and *E.T.* fame, was tapped to create the movie's soundtrack.

At first Rowling was concerned about the choice of an American screenwriter, Steve Kloves, who wrote and directed *The Fabulous Baker Boys.* When she met him, however, Kloves told Rowling that his favorite character was Hermione. That immediately put Rowling at ease, since she had infused Hermione with so much of her own personality.

The movie was scheduled for release on November 16, 2001. Eager fans could view the trailer online as of March 2001, and filming wrapped up in April. Only the finishing touches and editing remained, such as the special effects for Quidditch games, to be rendered by George Lucas's computer animation company, Industrial Light and Magic. Rowling, who was treated to a sneak preview of the footage, described the film as "fantastic." She has warned that despite the rumors, Book Five will not be released to coincide with the movie. In fact, it most likely will not be published until 2002. In the meantime, the movies will attempt to catch up with the books—filming on *Harry Potter and the Chamber of Secrets* was planned to begin in summer 2001. As with the books, there will be two different versions of the movies: one version for Brits and another with more-distilled Briticisms for American consumption.

More than just the Harry Potter movie has been taken out of Rowling's hands. Legally the Harry Potter juggernaut has a life all its own. The lawyers arrived in November 1999, when Rowling, Scholastic, and Time Warner filed suit in New York against Nancy K. Stouffer of Camp Hill, Pennsylvania. Stouffer had contacted Time Warner and Scholastic with claims that the Harry Potter books infringed on the copyright and trademarks of her 1984 book, *The Legend of Rah and the Muggles.* The suit, which sought a court declaration that Scholastic, Rowling, and Time Warner had not violated any copyrights or trademarks, was filed after the parties failed to reach an out-of-court settlement. In March 2000, Nancy Stouffer filed a countersuit in Pennsylvania, alleging copyright and trademark violations.

Stouffer and her lawyer, Kevin Casey, appeared on an episode of CNN's *Burden of Proof* on July 5, 2000, to explain their point of view. In Stouffer's book "muggles" are small, blue, hairless creatures that take in two orphaned boys. Although they are quite different from Rowling's Muggles—her word for regular, nonmagical people— Stouffer argues that the Harry Potter books' aggressive use of the word *Muggle* makes it impossible for her to market her books and intellectual property, resulting in unfair trade practices. She also alleges other similarities between the books: Stouffer has characters named Larry and Lilly Potter; Rowling has a Harry and a Lily Potter. And there are additional minor similarities: both books have a character called the Keeper of the Keys—although in the Harry Potter books this title for Hagrid has significance only in Book One and is soon forgotten thereafter—and several other terms in common, such as Nimbus (a brand of racing broom in Harry's world). Although Stouffer claims to have defended her "muggle" trademark successfully twice before, hers is a common-law trademark, based on use, rather than a federal trademark, which has slightly greater significance under the law. In addition, her books were out of print throughout most of the 1990s and did not reappear until May 2001.

In response to Stouffer's claims, Scholastic issued this statement: "Ms. Rowling's creative mind works in a world filled with myths and legends, but let there be no doubt that these books are her unique creations. Unfortunately, nowadays, success seems to breed not only imitation but also litigation."

Stouffer alleges that Rowling could have encountered her books in Europe in 1987 at the Nuremberg Book Fair, at a bookshop in London that had expressed interest in Stouffer's books, or as a work-study student in Baltimore in the late 1980s. Rowling, however, has always maintained that she never visited the United States prior to her book tours to promote Harry Potter. The dispute should be resolved in 2001; in August 2000 a judge ruled that the case should be heard in Manhattan, clearing the way for the trial to be scheduled.

Lawyers have been active in other areas as well. In December 2000, Warner Brothers began aggressively clamping down on fan websites sporting Harry Potter–derived domain names. In one particular case the company's action seemed justified. On December 21, 2000, the United Nations' World Intellectual Property Organization granted Time Warner Entertainment the rights to 107 domain names, all of which had been registered by Harper Stephens of Agoura Hills, California. Time Warner pointed out that most of the names had been registered a mere two days after a press release announcing that a Harry Potter movie was forthcoming, and none of the domain names showed active sites.

Time Warner's other Internet battles are not as cut-and-dried. The company enraged legions of fans when its lawyers sent letters to hundreds of people operating Harry

*Nancy Stouffer believes Harry Potter has infringed on her copyright and trademarks of her 1984 book* The Legend of Rah and the Muggles. *As of summer 2001, the outcome of the case remained uncertain.*

Potter fan sites, asking them to remove their pages and turn over the domain names to the company. Although some complied for fear of an expensive court battle, others refused to back down. Still, many of those fighting the company removed photos and images from their sites to comply with copyright and trademark regulations. By summer 2001 fans had something to cheer about: in the face of organized and vehement opposition, Time Warner had abandoned its campaign.·

Even J. K. Rowling herself is not immune to being pushed around by Time Warner's lawyers. In October 2000, to the delight of the students, Rowling gave permission to the North Foreland Lodge School, a British all-girls boarding school, to put on the first dramatic production of *Harry Potter and the Philosopher's Stone.* Two members of the school's faculty adapted the play, and the excited Harry-to-be, Charlotte Bailey, was interviewed for an article in the October 7, 2000, edition of the *London Times*. Unfortunately, the students' joy was short lived. Although Rowling felt that the private, not-for-profit nature of the schoolgirls' play was not in conflict with the seven-year moratorium on Harry Potter productions required by her agreement with Warner Brothers, the lawyers disagreed. Under pressure from Time Warner's lawyers, Rowling was forced to retract permission for the play only a few weeks later. She apologized profusely to the school for the mistake and arranged to visit the school to help make up for the disappointment.

It's not just the lawyers with whom Rowling doesn't see eye to eye. Although she and her agent did sell the merchandising rights to Time Warner in October 1999, she isn't eager to see Harry Potter become the ultimate marketing machine. "I would do anything to prevent Harry from turning up in fast-food boxes everywhere," she said in a July 10, 2000, interview with the *New York Times*. "That would be my worst nightmare."

Her nightmare may be coming true, and there probably isn't anything she can do to prevent it. Warner Brothers licensed some merchandising rights to Mattel, Hasbro, and Bloomsbury Publishing in England, and chose Electronic Arts to develop a Harry Potter video game. By Christmas 2000 numerous products had arrived, with more following in the spring of 2001. It wasn't long before stores were carrying Hogwarts journals, stickers, bookmarks, and throw pillows; Harry Potter board games; and bags of Bertie Bott's Every Flavor beans (thanks to Jelly Belly, maker of gourmet jelly beans). There is some hope, however, that children and their parents won't be overwhelmed by cheap Harry Potter trinkets. Warner Brothers included Rowling in meetings to discuss merchandising strategies. And according to an article in the August 9, 1999, issue of *Business Weekly,* Scholastic and Warner Brothers were in agreement

*The first Harry Potter products arrived on the shelves in time for Christmas 2000. Pictured is the* Harry Potter Book of Spells—*a personal organizer for the young wizard who has everything.*

that Harry Potter should be treated as an "enduring classic," with merchandise carefully controlled to protect the brand. "We are very conscious of quality," said a Warner Brothers spokesman. Rowling has agent Christopher Little firmly on her side as well. "No one wants to see the brand cheapened," he said.

The blockbuster products wouldn't arrive until later in 2001. Wizards of the Coast, a subsidiary of Hasbro, released a trading-card game based on the first book in August 2001. The collectible card game was similar in design to the company's best-selling *Pokemon* and *Magic: The Gathering* card games, featuring cards of varying rarities with original art. In the multiplayer game each player is a wizard at Hogwarts and tries to use his or her spell, potion, and creature cards to eliminate all of the other players' cards from the game.

In November 2001, Electronic Arts planned to release the first version of the Harry Potter video game to coincide with the release of the Harry Potter movie. The game was initially designed for four platforms: Game Boy Color, Game Boy Advance, PlayStation, and IBM-compatible personal computers. Versions for brand-new console game platforms PlayStation 2, Gamecube, and Xbox were scheduled for release the following year. The designers worked closely with J. K. Rowling, asking her for details on the rules of Quidditch and making certain that the game stayed true to the spirit of the books. Eager fans will get to be Harry himself, slowly learning new powers at Hogwarts until the ultimate confrontation with Voldemort. Unlike most video games, nothing gets blown up with massive weapons, and Harry can't die. Rowling, not a video-game fan, is relieved that the game isn't lethal. "I do have a real problem with gratuitous violence. . . . My daughter doesn't have a PlayStation at the moment. She is desperate for one. . . . I don't like the idea that they're going to be blowing people up . . . with no thought of what this really means. And doing that for points." She told Electronic Arts' game designers, "Thanks for not giving Harry an M16."

All of these products and the movie should be enough to keep Harry Potter mania stoked until *Harry Potter and the Order of the Phoenix* arrives on bookshelves. With Jessica Rowling nagging her mother daily to finish the book so she can find out what happens next, perhaps fans won't have too long a wait.

Of course, the mass marketing of Harry Potter hasn't been all bad for J. K. Rowling. She has become one of the best-known authors in the world. Her books have been translated into 42 different languages, with more than 100 million copies sold worldwide. She has appeared on the cover and between the pages of numerous magazines and was a compelling runner-up for *Time* magazine's Person of the Year award for 2000. And, not surprisingly, she has become one of the wealthiest women in the United Kingdom, earning between $30 million and $40 million a year.

She makes no secret of being uncomfortable with her success. "Sometimes I think I'm temperamentally suited to being a moderately successful writer," she said in *Telling Tales*. "There are times . . . when I would gladly give back some of the money in exchange for time and peace to write." On the other hand, she is tremendously grateful that Harry Potter's success has given her the financial means to continue writing without ever needing to worry about money again. "The main thing is this profound feeling of relief. I no longer have the constant worry of whether [Jessica] will outgrow a pair of shoes before I've got the money for the next pair," she told the *London Telegraph*.

In spite of her enormous wealth, Rowling tries to lead a "mundane" life. Like other British and Scottish parents, she takes her daughter to school in the morning and picks her up in the afternoon (although a nanny takes care of that job two days a week to give Rowling more time to write); she makes afternoon tea; and she cares for the family pets—a guinea pig named Jasmine, a "mad and violent" rabbit named Jemima, and, of course, some tropical fish. She also takes time to watch her favorite television show, the hit British comedy *The Royle Family,* about the daily life of a rather crass lower-class family. And despite her access to technology and secretarial help, she still prefers to write the first draft of each book in longhand—in cafés, of course—and then revise it while typing it into her laptop computer herself.

Rowling hasn't given much thought to what she will do after she finishes the Harry Potter series. She has a filing cabinet full of notes for various works of adult fiction but fears she'll think they're "rubbish" when she finally gets a chance to look through them. But, she said in *Telling Tales,* "I'm sure I'll always write, at least until I lose my marbles."

# CHRONOLOGY

**1965**  Joanne Rowling is born July 31 in Chipping Sodbury, to Peter and Anne Rowling.

**1967**  Dianne Rowling is born.

**1974**  The Rowlings move to Tutshill, near Chepstow, in Wales.

**1976**  Joanne enters Wyedean Comprehensive School in Chepstow.

**1979**  Joanne reads *Hons and Rebels,* by Jessica Mitford.

**1980**  Anne Rowling is diagnosed with multiple sclerosis.

**1983**  Joanne graduates with honors from Wyedean Comprehensive, as Head Girl; she enrolls at the University of Exeter.

**1987**  Graduates from Exeter with a degree in French and classics.

**1990**  Dreams up Harry Potter and Hogwarts on a train ride between Manchester and London. Begins work on *Harry Potter and the Philosopher's Stone.* Moves to Manchester to join boyfriend. Mother dies of multiple sclerosis.

**1991**  Moves to Oporto, Portugal, to teach English as a second language.

**1992**  Marries Jorge Arantes, a Portuguese television journalist.

**1993**  Jessica is born; Joanne leaves Jorge and moves to Edinburgh, Scotland.

**1994**  Rowling is forced to accept public assistance in order to care for Jessica while finishing *Harry Potter and the Philosopher's Stone.*

**1995**  Rowling finishes *Philosopher's Stone*; agent Christopher Little agrees to represent the novel.

**1996**  Bloomsbury Publishing offers more than $3,000 for the right to publish *Harry Potter and the Philosopher's Stone.*

**1997**  Rowling receives a $13,000 grant from the Scottish Arts Council to work on *Harry Potter and the Chamber of Secrets. Harry Potter and the Philosopher's Stone* is published in July, receives good reviews. Scholastic buys the American rights to *Philosopher's Stone* for $105,000. *Philosopher's Stone* wins the Nestlé Smarties prize in November, begins flying off bookshelves.

**1998**  *Philosopher's Stone* wins the British Book Awards Children's Book of the Year. *Harry Potter and the Chamber of Secrets* is released in Britain in July; both Harry Potter books are at the top of best-seller lists. The first book, with the title changed to *Harry Potter and the Sorcerer's Stone,* is released in the United States in September. Rowling sells movie rights to Warner Brothers.

**1999**    The American version of *Chamber of Secrets* is released in June. The third book, *Harry Potter and the Prisoner of Azkaban,* is released in Britain in July and in the United States in September. All three Harry Potter books top best-seller lists. Rowling sells merchandising rights to Warner Brothers, tours U.S. in October.

**2000**    *Harry Potter and the Goblet of Fire* is released in Britain, Canada, and the U.S. simultaneously. Days later the *New York Times* creates children's best-seller list and moves Potter books onto it. Christopher Little announces Book Five won't be released until 2002.

**2001**    *Quidditch Through the Ages* and *Fantastic Beasts and Where to Find Them* are released in March to benefit British charity Comic Relief. The movie version of *Harry Potter and the Sorcerer's Stone* hits theaters on November 16.

# FURTHER READING

**Books and Magazine Articles**

Bouquet, Tim. "The Wizard Behind Harry Potter." *Reader's Digest,* December 2000.

Feldman, Roxanne. "The Truth About Harry." *School Library Journal,* September 1, 1999.

Frasier, Lindsey. *Telling Tales: An Interview with J. K. Rowling.* London: Mammoth, 2000.

Gray, Paul. "The Magic of Potter." *Time,* December 25, 2000.

————. "Wild About Harry." *Time*, September 20, 1999.

Ratnesar, Romesh. "Inside the Halls of Hogwarts." *ON Magazine*, June 2001.

Rowling, J. K. "A Good Scare." *Time*, October 30, 2000.

"Rowling Reveals Secrets of Her Success." *USA Today,* July 9, 2000.

Shapiro, Marc. *J. K. Rowling: The Wizard Behind Harry Potter.* New York: St. Martin's Griffin, 2000.

Weir, Margaret. "Of Magic and Single Motherhood." *Salon,* March 31, 1999.

**Websites**

Bloomsbury Publishing
  *www.bloomsbury.com/harrypotter*

Harry Potter Movie Site
  *www.harrypotter.warnerbrothers.com*

Harry Potter Network
  *www.hpnetwork.f2s.com*

J. K. Rowling on the Web
  *www.ksu.edu/english/nelp/rowling/index.html*

Scholastic Press
  *www.scholastic.com*

Stories from the Web
  *www.hosted.ukoln.ac.uk/stories/stories/rowling/interview.htm*

The Unofficial Harry Potter Fan Club
  *www.harrypotterfans.net*

**Works by J. K. Rowling**

*Harry Potter and the Sorcerer's Stone,* 1998

*Harry Potter and the Chamber of Secrets,* 1999

*Harry Potter and the Prisoner of Azkaban,* 1999

*Harry Potter and the Goblet of Fire,* 2000

*Fantastic Beasts and Where to Find Them* (Newt Scamander, pseud.), 2001

*Quidditch Through the Ages* (Kennilworthy Whisp, pseud.), 2001

# INDEX

# PICTURE CREDITS

**Lisa A. Chippendale** is a freelance editor, writer, and violinist. She has worked in a variety of publishing genres, including magazines, scientific journals, websites, books, and children's fiction. Ms. Chippendale is also the author of *The San Francisco Earthquake of 1906* in Chelsea House's GREAT DISASTERS: REFORMS AND RAMIFICATIONS series. She lives outside Philadelphia with her husband, Ross Beauchamp, a freelance cello player and teacher.

**James Scott Brady** serves on the board of trustees with the Center to Prevent Handgun Violence and is the vice chairman of the Brain Injury Foundation. Mr. Brady served as assistant to the President and White House press secretary under President Ronald Reagan. He was severely injured in an assassination attempt on the president, but remained the White House press secretary until the end of the administration. Since leaving the White House, Mr. Brady has lobbied for stronger gun laws. In November 1993, President Bill Clinton signed the Brady Bill, a national law requiring a waiting period on handgun purchases and a background check on buyers.